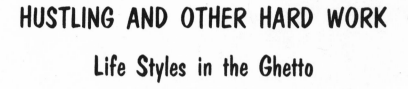

HUSTLING AND OTHER HARD WORK

Life Styles in the Ghetto

by Bettylou Valentine

THE FREE PRESS

A Division of Macmillan Publishing Co., Inc.

NEW YORK

THE FREE PRESS
A Division of Macmillan Publishing Co., Inc.
866 Third Avenue, New York, N.Y. 10022

Collier Macmillan Canada, Ltd.

Library of Congress Catalog Card Number: 78-427

Printed in the United States of America

printing number — hardbound edition

2 3 4 5 6 7 8 9 10

printing number — paperback edition

4 5 6 7 8 9 10

Library of Congress Cataloging in Publication Data

Valentine, Bettylou
    Hustling and other hard work.

    Bibliography: p.
    Includes index.
    1. Afro–Americans—Economic conditions.
2. Afro–Americans—Social conditions—1975–
I. Title.
E185.8.V25   330.9'73   78–427
ISBN 0-02-933060-2 (hardbound)
ISBN 0-02-933070-X (paperback)

To Val and Reggie,
who made this book
possible and necessary

CONTENTS

PREFACE

THE PEOPLE WHO live in the ghetto of "Blackston" had a deep impact on me as a person, as an Afro-American, as a woman, and as one who has known poverty. These were my people, and I learned far more from them about the realities of being Black and poor than I had learned from thirty years of living in other kinds of communities, travel in the United States and Europe, higher education, and the news media and expert writings on similar communities. On the surface Blackston appeared much as popular and learned views portray such places and their people. Although I mistrusted these views and their sources, the world outside the many Blackstons provided no solid basis for challenging those portrayals. Five years of living among Blackstonians deeply convinced me that under the surface is an entirely different reality. I wanted very much to describe this reality and to explore why so much that is said and written about my people is at odds with my own new-found knowledge. The result is this book.

The National Science Foundation provided generous and unrestricted support (GS-3237) to the research that forms the basis of this report. The Bureau of the Census gave early and continuing support by funding a special substudy. Contractual obligations require the citation of National Institute of Mental Health grant MH 16866-01.

A number of individuals have been supportive and constructively critical of this work as it developed, including Johnnetta Cole, Robert Hoppock, Rose Marie Jaquith, Beryl Malawsky, Laura Scanlon, Eleanor M. Schetlin, and Clara Rodriquez. My son, Jonathan Ragi, has been a help and a delight during the research and writing. Charles A. Valentine, my co-investigator, husband, friend, and colleague, contributed most to this writing.

The Burtons, the Wards, and the Wilsons, and the many other people of Blackston, deserve special thanks for letting me share their lives. I hope that my desire to improve conditions for all Blackston residents through fuller knowledge and understanding of their present situation justifies the exposure of their lives to public view.

INTRODUCTION

BY CHARLES A. VALENTINE

THIS BOOK IS ABOUT the everyday lives of real people. It comes to conclusions that challenge widely held beliefs. It is based on expert and extended study but has not been written only for specialists or students. The author wants her work to reach ordinary readers and addresses herself to people whose lives are like those described in the book. Believing she has learned most from common people, she feels that they have at least an equal right to know what she has found.

The people described in *Hustling and Other Hard Work* are Afro-Americans. They are ordinary Black people living in one of the poorest parts of a big city in the northern United States during the 1960s and 1970s. To protect their privacy the author gave the place where they live the name Blackston, gave every person a new name, and disguised personal details that would have been easy to recognize and were unimportant anyway.

The lives described here were lived with little money and few possessions. The condition of the buildings, blocks, and neighborhoods in which these human beings existed ranged from bad to worse. The surrounding city supplied only the poorest services of all kinds. When the outside world was aware of Blackston at all, it granted little or no respect to Blackstonians, and the people themselves sometimes found it hard to maintain self-respect. They lived in what they and outsiders alike called a ghetto and a slum. Yet their home was also a community with its own real name, organizations, and special qualities.

The problem of making a living was the basic one in the lives of the characters in this book. In her account of their lives, the

1

author shows the difficulties the people faced and the threefold solution they worked out. Finding the jobs open to them scarce, poorly paid, unreliable, and often degrading, Blackstonians combined jobs with two other kinds of hard work: "welfare" and hustling. Getting whatever one can from the various agencies for so-called welfare is a much harder task, less predictable, and less rewarding than those who have not had to do it recognize. To complete the strategy there is hustling, which in the ghetto means a great variety of officially disapproved activities, including many kinds of stealing as well as "wheeling and dealing" in illegal goods and services. Seldom more profitable to the individual or more reliable than the others, this way is also often more dangerous.

In the actual flow of real lives, these approaches blend into a complex and shifting pattern. Blackston families normally make use of all three kinds of resources, in combinations that vary from person to person and from time to time. No part of the pattern is free and easy, simple or secure.

On this basis Blackstonians build their families and homes, their neighborhoods and community organizations. Within this framework children grow up, marriages and other matings are made and dissolved, relatives cooperate and quarrel, and people find ways to have fun, to hope and dream, *and* to take group action for changing their world. This book shows plainly how people surmount the struggle for survival to live lives filled with a truly human mixture of strength and weakness, triumphs and unsolved problems, creativity and routine. It reports how those who are both Black and poor persist in being human despite inhumane conditions.

These patterns are not portrayed here by catalogs of statistics, clinical reports, or abstract descriptions. Instead, the author tells the stories of human lives as she experienced them by being a part of them. Her accounts center on three groupings of people who were related to one another through family ties, friendship, neighborliness, and various networks in everyday life. These particular sets of people were chosen because they represented the range and variety of human responses to the conditions of existence in Blackston.

Bettylou Valentine was born Betty Lou Burleigh in 1937. She is an Afro-American from Pittsburgh, far from Blackston. Her family was poor but respectable, as was the area where they lived. Though some blocks of private homes and a nearby public housing project were divided into Black and White sections, the district as a whole was not restricted to one race or another. The Burleighs and the other inhabitants did not think of their neighborhood as either a ghetto or a slum.

Bettylou was the only member of her family lucky enough to go to college. This was at the University of Pittsburgh, where she earned a bachelor's degree in psychology. During her college years, she entered vigorously into the civil rights movement and into radical political organizations, trying to change society in the interests of her own people and the poor in general. Ever since, she has been at least as much a political person as a scholar.

For graduate study she moved to the University of Washington at Seattle, from which in 1961 she received a master's degree in anthropology. In this and related social sciences she found knowledge, ideas, and methods of study that could help her understand the ways in which varied groups of people live. Though critical of these fields for their general support of the existing order ruling society, she felt she could use something from them to discover the shape of social reality in order to work toward changing it.

Before beginning the work leading directly to this book, Bettylou had much experience with other communities of minority and poor people. During and after her own training, she herself taught Black students in a variety of institutions from the East Coast to the West. She also worked at a professional job in a so-called antipoverty agency in St. Louis for over a year. Yet she had never lived full-time for a lengthy period in a ghetto.

Meanwhile Bettylou married an anthropology professor named Valentine who came from a family that considered itself free, White, and unjustly poor. His ideas and interests were and are very much like her own. Shared outlooks led to questions about mutual concerns. Why is poverty so persistent in the United States? Why is this burden borne so disproportionately by Afro-Americans and other minorities? What are the sources of this enduring inequality?

The usual answers were not convincing. Either they did not

square with evidence and experience, or they were clearly biased against attempts to change society radically toward equality. Conservative politicians argued that inequality was the natural order of things, that radical change was impossible or destructive. Liberals proclaimed that the injustices of the past were being overcome, things were getting better for those who had been least favored, and pushing "too hard" would only hold back natural progress. Expert and scholarly judgments were expressed in different words, but their basic meaning was the same. A common theme of many learned opinions was that inequality stemmed from defects in the poor themselves. Some said the source was biological and was reflected in low intelligence and poor character. Some called it social or psychological but still found the causes in the poor—in weak minds, sick personalities, disordered families, group habits of depending on support rather than making an effort, whole ways of life supposedly peculiar to the poor that allegedly keep them in their lowly position.

All this neatly fitted the prejudices of a class-ridden racist society and supported the interests and positions of the rich and powerful, who benefit most from the existing system. A search for better answers might well begin by carefully comparing this concept of group defects with a fresh body of facts and experience. Would the notion that weaknesses in the lower classes keep them poor stand up against a searching study of how a community of people in this position actually live?

It should be possible to use methods from anthropology and related fields like sociology to investigate this question. Yet it would be necessary to prevent these methods, together with their framework of ideas and grounding in political philosophy, from biasing and distorting the work by simply reproducing accepted answers. The facts must speak for themselves, whether they confirmed old theories, demanded changes in present ideas, or led to new conclusions. For this purpose the study must be more direct and realistic than previous research. It must be based solidly on experience of material conditions and the actual practice of social life.

So in 1968 Bettylou Valentine, with her husband and one-year-old son, went to live in Blackston. It was chosen over other places because it was the right kind of community for the planned study and because it was far away from personal and professional ties that might be a distraction from the work. The purpose of the move was for the family to become as much a part of the whole Blackston scene as was humanly possible.

For the next five years we did just that. We really became Blackstonians, though for several main reasons we were never typical of its citizens. First, there were unchangeable aspects of our backgrounds, such as nonghetto childhoods and university experiences, which were not shared by many or most of our neighbors. Second, we took part in the life of the community more intensely than many of its members did because as we lived it we were also studying it. Equally important, we could leave the ghetto to continue our lives elsewhere, which most Blackstonians could *not* do.

During the first year the family lived on half of one university salary. This was a quarter of our previous family income and brought us within the range of Blackston incomes. Later there were temporary grants of money from research agencies to support our work. During the final six months we restricted our income to the same level as the meager public assistance that is misnamed welfare.

For five years we inhabited the same decrepit, rat- and roach-infested buildings as everyone else, lived on the same poor-quality food at inflated prices, trusted our health and our son's schooling to the same inferior institutions, suffered the same brutality and intimidation from the police, and like others made the best of it by some combination of endurance, escapism, and fighting back. Like the dwellings of neighbors, our home went up in flames several times, including one disaster caused by the carelessness or ill will of the city's "firefighters." For several cold months we lived and worked in one room without heat other than what a cooking stove could provide, without hot water or windows, and with only one light bulb.

The family took part in all kinds of organized and spontaneous community activities, from church services to protest demonstrations. The work ranged from attending many public events to exploring all possible institutions to regularly observing everyday life in homes and on the street. Meanwhile, we came to know a great many people extremely well, constantly visited back and forth with neighbors and others throughout the community, and learned much about the private lives of many Blackstonians. With neighbors and others we shared everything from babysitting and food to entertainment and spare sleeping space. Friendships were many, and there were enmities too. We became adopted relatives, had quarrels, made up, took part in many an argument and discussion of the world, shared the cares of Blackston life, and reveled in the dancing, partying, and other forms of fun-making that do so much to relieve the tensions of ghetto existence. To a far greater extent than is possible for most people, life and work were a unity for us. We lived our work and labored lovingly at making our lives fulfill the plan that brought us to Blackston.

All this was possible because the people of Blackston accepted us for what we were. We made sure that everyone with whom we had contact knew what we were doing and what our purposes were. They in turn made sure by their own observations, and by testing us through practice, that we were real neighbors and genuine participants in community life.

During these years Blackston had its share of both spontaneous insurrections and the revolutionary organizations that expressed the ghetto's anguish at the time. Before the family moved to Blackston, there had been many warnings from university people that our study would be impossible because of Black anger and hostility against snooping outsiders. We were told that as an interracial couple we would be in danger of our lives. In one way or another we were close to a great many group conflicts that took place in and near Blackston. There were quite real dangers, and indeed we suffered some painful injuries, from outsiders such as the police. Yet we never felt threatened by Blackstonians or their allies from other ghettos. Everyone knew we were not only *in* the community but *of* it and *for* its people.

Different ways of inquiring into people's lives may also inspire either confidence or distrust. We relied first of all on direct observation and shared experience. We paid close attention to whatever people told us of their own accord. Only when people showed that they were ready for it did we ask questions and then only little by little as trust developed on both sides. Our willingness to satisfy their curiosity about us helped give a mutual quality to our working relations with Blackstonians. This included many discussions of our purposes, our ways of going about the work, and what was being found as we went along.

Certain parts of this work were especially Bettylou's own. One of her main interests was the people's everyday life at home, on the blocks, in the neighborhoods. She experienced deeply the problems of how children are brought up, how men and women come together and part, how family members relate to one another—and how people gain the livelihoods to make all this possible. She spent a great deal of time directly observing and taking part in relations between Blackstonians and the many institutions controlled from outside the community: retail stores, schools, hospitals, welfare agencies, jails and prisons, and more.

Throughout this experience she kept asking herself particular questions that flowed from the general problems that had brought her to Blackston. Do Blackstonians remain poor because they are unable or unwilling to put forth a normal amount of human effort? Do they accept welfare and practice hustling because they know nothing else, want nothing else, and are content with the results? Is there an overall life style that Blackstonians in general follow and that keeps them where they are? Are families disorganized and unable to support individuals or provide a genuine home life? Are the people ignorant of the cultural values expressed by the more successful classes and opposed to consistent social practices? Have dependence on welfare and reliance on hustling become built-in social habits that keep people immobilized? One of the primary purposes of this book is to find answers to these and similar questions in the lives of individuals and families within a community.

After leaving Blackston in 1973, Bettylou Valentine took another university job, again far away from our favorite ghetto, this time as a dean and lecturer in health sciences at the State University of New York at Stony Brook. At this time she began writing an early version of *Hustling and Other Hard Work*. This was to be a doctoral thesis for yet another graduate school, and in 1975 the author duly received her Ph.D. in anthropology from the Union Graduate School at Antioch, Ohio. Finally, that manuscript was revised for publication as the present book.

The way in which some of the most important final revisions were made is another of Bettylou Valentine's own special contributions to the project from which her book has come. She persuaded a number of the subjects of this volume to take part in shaping its final form. This important and unusual step was taken because of the author's respect for the people described and for their interests. She also respects the ability of these people, as readers, to follow and respond to what she has written. This is based partly on the fact that most of the people who have large parts in these life stories read the book before it was printed, understood it, appreciated it, and finally made their own direct contributions to the published version.

The author arranged for each major character in the book to receive a copy of the manuscript, asked them to read it, and requested them to comment and to suggest any changes they might want before the work was published. She then visited and revisited Blackston for lengthy discussions of these questions. Everyone confirmed the descriptions and factual sections, except for a few unimportant details, which have been corrected. All who discussed the manuscript agreed with the conclusions. Some expressed anxieties about personal exposure as a result of publication, and so additional disguises were worked out for individually revealing but generally unimportant details.

The organization of this book is simple and straightforward; most of the writing is nontechnical. First comes "The Setting," a chapter describing Blackston as a community. Next is the main body of the work, headed "The People"; it recounts the life stories of three extended families, or sets of closely related families, and their friends, neighbors, and associates. Then in a chapter titled "The Meaning," the author presents her conclusions about the questions that stimulated the work.

The last two chapters are somewhat more specialized. They deal with methods used and results produced by other writers in their studies of other Black communities, comparing these with what was done in Blackston. "Other Views" defines the method of ethnography as the Blackston team tried to use it. Quotations from experts in the field show how the class system and racial biases of White America work through the social sciences to prevent this approach from being applied frequently or fully in studies of Black people. The author shows briefly how similar forces produce both the appeal and the weaknesses of the more usual census and survey approaches. Most of this chapter explores the work of some dozen researchers in order to identify their failures and successes in attempting or claiming to use ethnographic method. This evaluation is made against the standard of a method that combines observing people's behavior under actual social conditions, participating in their collective life, and questioning groups or individuals in order to understand their community or their kind of community.

"The Design" completes the book by describing in detail some of the main methods we used in Blackston in hopes of overcoming the weaknesses of earlier studies. Greatest attention is given here to how information on the community can be collected and combined from different perspectives and how people being studied can make active contributions to the work right up to its final stages. To make all this meaningful, the author relates many concrete details of how she and her family lived and worked in Blackston.

The author calls the message of her work its thesis. This thesis includes several points that are argued in the book and supported by many facts. In order to survive in Blackston and similar places, people must work, people must hustle, and people must take welfare. People like Blackstonians must do all these things together in varying combinations all their lives. It follows that Black and poor people in ghettos have created and follow life styles that are more the result of poverty than its cause. These life styles include skills and values that most outsiders believe belong only to the White working and middle classes. Afro-American ways are greatly influenced and limited by the poverty that society imposes on Black communities. Beliefs held outside the ghettos and descriptions made by authors not from the ghettos are false or incomplete if they do not include these points. These are the main answers Bettylou Valentine found to the questions she started out with. Most ghetto people know these things. If ghetto people can see these points set forth in a book, and if other people can learn and understand this message, *Hustling and Other Hard Work* will have served its purpose. I believe both the book and its readers will succeed in this.

As this book comes out and is appreciated, it will become clear that Afro-Americans—like all other collections of human beings—have defects, lacks, and weaknesses as well as strengths and virtues. Yet it will be equally clear that the main causes of this people's poverty cannot be found in their collective or individual deficiencies as human beings. It will also be recognized, of course, that the people's strengths have not yet been enough to overcome or overthrow the forces that do cause poverty, especially non-White poverty.

So, the main sources of poverty are not in the poor, their behavior, their mentalities, or their values. The major sources arise outside the ghettos, in the economic and political forces or processes of the society as a whole. Much about how these forces create and perpetuate Black poverty is revealed in this book. It is thus a basic source for understanding how these processes work. Why this kind of society imposes poverty on people is clearly implied here, but it is not the aim of this particular book to spell this out.

By the time this book is read, the particular Blackston described here will probably be gone. It will most likely have been wiped out by blight, urban renewal, or possibly even revolution. Still, for every Blackston that dies, several more are born and grow. Even without a Blackston, there will long be Blackstonians, their children, and their children's children. Now the newer Blackstons and the younger Blackstonians will benefit more than before from the experiences and stories of the older ones.

THE SETTING

BLACKSTON IS A named district of a large northern city. It is thought of as a community by most of the people who live there. The eastern boundary is a railroad embankment that separates Blackston from a neighboring low-income ghetto populated mostly by Puerto Ricans. A major city highway forms the northern limit. Beyond it is another low-income Black and Hispanic community with a distinct identity, but with common interests. These two communities sometimes join to act on such issues as education and poverty programs. In the southern and western sections of Blackston are several blocks of two-family houses, many of them in moderate to good states of repair. Many of these buildings are owner-occupied, unlike the tenements where most Blackston people live. These tenements were built in the early 1900s for immigrants from Eastern Europe, poor people who lived in a community that even then was described as drab, dismal, congested, and noisy. Centrally located within the area are several large units of public housing, where some 20,000 to 25,000 people, about one-quarter of Blackston's population, live. This public housing is relatively new, most of it built during the post–World War II boom, some more recently. A small industrial strip—consisting of a steel mill, toy and clothing factories, box makers, and other light and medium industries—separates Blackston's southern portion from a middle- and working-class White community, with which part of Blackston shares the services of an almost all-White police precinct. Public services and public facilities such as postal area, police precincts, school districts, municipal health areas, and electoral districts, which are determined by city, state, and federal governments, cut across community boundaries in arbitrary ways.

Blackston residents are well aware of the sharp contrast be-

11

tween their community and the surrounding areas in housing conditions, housing discrimination, school plant and curriculum, employment opportunities, and income levels. During particular crises involving such issues as quality education/integration, police brutality, or welfare crackdowns, Blackston residents voiced their awareness that their social services were determined by, and policies decided by, people outside their community. At such times, the people who knew our role as writers asked me to "tell it like it is." To do that I had to describe the physical and social setting in some detail—and more important, remind the reader that Blackston is not an isolated, self-sufficient, self-determining community but a part of the larger American society.

PHYSICAL SCENE. Blackston has often been described in the media as resembling Dresden after the infamous Allied bombing of that city—empty, burned-out buildings; lots filled with loose bricks, rubble, rubbish, and rats. City officials refer to it as "the fastest-decaying residential area of the city." Bright patches of lead-based pastel paint dot the landscape where one of two adjoining buildings has been torn down. In the cheaply constructed housing, two buildings often share a center wall, and so the kitchen, hall, bedroom, and living-room walls of the demolished building remain to add splashes of color to the usual grays, browns, and blacks of the community. The walls thus revealed to public view are so similar to those in occupied tenements that it is easy to imagine one's own walls being bared to public view by the next swath of fire or slum clearance.

The tenement apartments are mostly four-room boxes in which the largest room is a kitchen whose single window opens onto a central courtlike airshaft that provides the only source of outside light for the front or back half of each apartment. The airshaft is shared by twelve or more apartments and is used mainly for clotheslines, which crisscross the area and are often full of clothes in winter as well as summer. If the winter weather is too cold, damp, or snowy to hang clothing outside, many Blackstonians drape their washing on the radiators, which are legally required to be in operation and provide heat for only four hours of the day and four hours of the night. Even this minimal heating requirement is frequently ignored by tenement landlords.

These apartments were built without closets and with minimal bathing facilities. It is often the plumbing that is in the worst state of repair after decades of use, and it is not unusual for an apartment to have a nonfunctioning toilet, cold water only, and pipes that drip continuously and that jut out of cracked, disintegrating plaster.

Census reports indicate that in 1960 two-thirds of the houses in the area where we lived were less than sound. Older residents and former residents describe the community as becoming more run-down and decayed in the past decade. During our five years in Blackston, from 1968 to 1973, at least thirty housing units on the single block where we lived were burned out, abandoned, or torn down.

Because many Blackston homes are without hot running water, a 10- or 12-quart pan of boiling water atop the kitchen gas stove is a common sight. A mother with a family who lives in an apartment with no running water—and there are many—obtains water from a neighbor or a fire hydrant in order to clean, cook, and otherwise care for her family, to flush toilets, and for many other activities that outsiders take for granted. In homes without heat, all the gas burners are continually left on at the highest flame possible, the oven is set on high, and the oven door is kept open. This means that only the kitchen may be warm enough to live in, and three or five or more people may be crowded into this one room. It also means that many people are forced to sleep at night with the stove burners flaming or with a portable electric heater set close to the bed in order to get its small warmth. With such hazards, fires are a constant threat. (Blackston has the highest fire rate of any section in the entire city.)

The oil burners, especially in the prewar buildings, are worn, often in need of major repair or relining, and continual attention. Such care is available only through the costly services of the local heating-oil companies. These companies refuse to deliver oil or to perform repairs at the residents' request or even in response to proffered cash payment from a tenant.

The whole issue of heat in winter is so enormous that the city provides emergency telephone numbers for residents to report problems. In theory the city will even attempt to provide emergency service or supplies while one section of the city bureaucracy attempts to use the records of another branch to identify, contact, and force the owner into doing what the law requires. Blackstonians we know who have used this city service have found it very unpredictable in terms of results: often the city records do not identify the true owner of the building; repair and emergency supply services are usually provided through local community poverty-manpower programs, which are overburdened and underfunded and therefore reach only a small percentage of those seeking help; the waiting period between first contact about a problem and action on that problem may be weeks, and very often nothing at all results from repeated calls. If lucky, the tenant may find another apartment in generally similar or even worse condition but whose major lack is something other than heat. So the heat-and-housing situation grows steadily worse in Blackston.

Despite the widespread sharing of word-of-mouth knowledge and suggestions about how to deal with external institutions, it is not possible to know all the legal complications, regulations, agency policies, and so forth. Thus a family may be burned out of a building on a cold winter night and be taken in by friendly and helpful neighbors, especially when children are involved. If the burned-out family does not notify the Red Cross within twenty-four hours, they are ineligible for any help from that organization. If the family spends the first postfire day trying to rescue items that have not been totally destroyed and does not get to the welfare department before 5 p.m., they may never even receive emergency shelter. Welfare department spokesmen take the position that the family evidently found emergency shelter and should just remain where they are. Bureaucratic reasoning ignores the likelihood that a family of three or four or more persons, willing to take an equal or larger number of fire victims into their small apartment for a day or two, cannot do so for the long period that may be involved while housing is found in a city with a massive and increasing housing shortage. The housing shortage is especially serious for non-Whites and Hispanics, who are excluded from many areas by racial discrimination.

POPULATION. A general picture of the Blackston population before and during the five years covered by this study (1968–1973) can be given on the basis of census figures, estimates by the local Blackston Community Council (BCC), and our own observations as involved social scientists.

According to public records, Blackston reached its largest size in the 1930s and its greatest concentration of a single ethnic group: 200,000 people, mainly Eastern European Jews. At that time the non-Jewish population of approximately 40,000 was evenly divided between Roman Catholic Italians and Protestants of varied European backgrounds. Although historical records mention at least one Afro-American family headed by a veteran of the Union Army settling in the Blackston area after the Civil War and a scattering of Blacks present in the community during the intervening years, it was not until after the Great Depression and into the early World War II years that Blacks became a substantial part of the community. According to the Bureau of the Census, the Black population was 2.5 percent of the Blackston total in 1930, 5 percent in 1940, 12 percent in 1950, almost 30 percent in 1960, and 71 percent in 1970. Meanwhile the Jewish population declined as people with rising incomes left the area and older settlers died off.

During the same period there has been a decline of the total population in the area. The total 1960 population of Blackston according to the census was about 100,000. In 1970 it was reported as 75,000. This decline in population is obviously related to a decline in suitable housing. Large sections of housing have been destroyed through slum clearance, accidental fires, or arson. A great many tenement buildings and family houses have been abandoned as unfit to live in.

A tiny handful of people are able to gather enough money from many sources to enable them to move into a less decayed area. Some Blackstonians are choosing to return to the South, but most of the Blackston population is being forced by lack of money and by discrimination into other ghetto areas within this huge city. In the next decade Blackston may cease to exist as a Black and Spanish community.

Today, the most obvious facet of Blackston beyond its physical deterioration is its multiethnic character. During the late 1960s and early 1970s Blackston was almost three-quarters Black and included southern- and northern-born Afro-Americans, as well as Black people from the West Indies, Haiti, South America, Cuba, and elsewhere. Approximately 25 percent of the population was Latin American, largely from Puerto Rico, but including people from Cuba, Brazil, and various other parts of Central and South America. There were also remnants of the Jewish and Italian populations that were once central to Blackston but now exist in sharply separate residential enclaves at the borders of the community. Finally there was a scattering of shopkeepers of Chinese and Arabic background, some Gypsies, and a few Amerindians.

The Blackston population is multiethnic and young. Almost 51 percent of the total Blackston population counted in the 1970 census was under eighteen years of age, compared with 34 percent of the total United States population. The preponderance of youth is evident, particularly in public places—on the street, in the stores, hanging out at shops and eating places, going to school, sitting on stoops.

Figures like these do not convey the flavor and excitement of standing at the intersection of the two major shopping streets of Blackston on welfare-check day, the first and fifteenth of each month, watching the lines of black, brown, beige, and cream-skinned people joking, smiling, calling to friends, while waiting to cash their checks and buy food stamps. At times like this, one becomes aware of the great diversity of physical types and language groups within what a casual observer would see only as a Black ghetto. The sight of so many men who come to help protect and to spend their women's money on check day makes one aware of the inaccuracy of census data, with their large categories of "missing men" and "fatherless households."

In the supermarkets of the area, the prices regularly go up on check days, but even this does not deter the women from stocking up on such basics as meat, rice, beans, greens, canned milk, and disposable diapers as well as whatever ethnically specialized items are desired and available. The service cars and privately owned automobiles that operate as taxis in this area of the city, where licensed taxis refuse (illegally) to pick up or bring passengers, also have an ethnic look. Many advertise their ethnic ownership by name or picture, and most sport bumper stickers stating: "We're not yellow, we go anywhere." On check day they line up outside the supermarkets and clothing stores while their drivers call out in Spanish, French patois, or locally accented Black English to attract customers.

Attending either of the two major Roman Catholic churches in the area, one notes the differences in appearance between the Irish Catholic priests and their largely Latin and Haitian parishioners. Blackston's Protestant churches range from solid, staid brick buildings, sometimes permanently marked with the six-pointed star of their previous owners, to storefront pentecostal-group buildings, often decorated with contact paper and hand-painted signs. There is also a Moorish Science Temple and a synagogue of the Black Israelites in the Blackston area.

Bare numbers do not reveal the alcoholic WASP leader of the Blackston Bible Mission, whose charge to convert the Jews to Christianity remains even though the Jewish population has left. "Captain" Larry therefore spends his time organizing the Black and Spanish elementary-school boys into paramilitary scoutlike groups and marching with them across the rubble-strewn lots and down the public thoroughfares.

One almost needs to be a linguist or to have been reared in a multicultural community to understand the dialects and strongly accented English spoken, for example, at a community council meeting by men whose clothing varies from coveralls to business suits and by women in miniskirts, slacks, or floor-length dresses worn for reasons of religion or fashion. Not only do people at these meetings understand each other, but they identify and try to place others in ethnic, class, and political categories on the basis of these features. Some Blackstonians feel that hair style or headdress—Afros, pressed-straightened hair, turbans, and less often wigs in many styles and colors—and clothing styles enable them to predict with a good degree of certainty the position of each speaker on a given issue. In addition, the community council is a place where some of the remaining Whites in or near the community interact with the Black and Spanish population of Blackston on a basis approaching equality and concerted joint activity rather than as landlord-tenant, proprietor-customer, professional-client, or employer-employee.

EMPLOYMENT AND UNEMPLOYMENT. The official unemployment rate for non-White males in 1970 showed that more than one out of ten Blackston men looking for a job was unable to find work. There were more than two Blackston men looking for work for each White man unable to find a job. In Blackston the actual rate was 12 percent for non-White males, compared with a national unemployment rate of 5 percent for White males. For many years, up to and including the present, the Black unemployment rate has been double that for Whites. Many analysts, including the National Urban League, which does its own survey and analysis of Black workers, feel that the Black unemployment figure would be more realistic and much higher if it included the many people in ghetto areas who are permanently unemployed, those who have not sought employment in the recent past because of discrimination and discouragement, as well as those missed by the survey method. During the period of the study, employment became steadily worse for Blackstonians. Blackston was cited in a 1970 federal government report on male unemployment. One finding of the study was that Blackston men in their prime employment years of twenty-five to fifty-four were three times as likely to be unemployed as men in the same age bracket elsewhere in the nation.

For women and youth the situation was even worse. As many as half of the young never-employed males were unable to find any job. Among women one out of each five searching for a job was unemployed.

Even within the employed categories, discrimination was evident. Blackston residents who are employed are generally faced with some combination of the following: steady but low-paid work in factories, hospitals, and other service areas; sporadic, unpredictable, or seasonal work that may pay a better wage, such as truck driving, construction labor, or dock work; or work that is both sporadic and low-paid.

A Census Bureau report issued in 1972 reports median family income for the entire subdivision of the metropolitan area that includes Blackston. For the subdivision it lists a range from "less than $6,000 to $18,000 and over." Every one of the fourteen census units in Blackston is in the lowest median income category: less than $6,000 per family per year.

The work available to most members of the Blackston community is unskilled, semiskilled, or minimally skilled industrial and service employment. Even this work is often temporary and transitory. There is also low-paid domestic work and a small percentage of clerical or sales jobs, particularly among the younger female population. In Blackston a male head of household with a wife and several children could and often did work full time at the legal minimum wage to earn a yearly income that amounted to half of what the Bureau of Labor Statistics sets as a "low" standard of living for a family of four. A "low" standard of living required nearly double the legal minimum wage in this area.

On the basis of our research, I would assert that there is very little refusal to work. The one important exception is young men and women who decline to accept the demeaning and minimally paid jobs that are typically available. It is hard to determine the proportion for whom this is true, for even people in this group may accept such work on occasion for a brief time, in order to earn money for some specific item or event. These include the young adult males one finds gathered in groups on the corner or stoop, sometimes drinking beer or wine from a communal container wrapped in a brown paper bag, talking, exchanging ideas on how to make money in some other way than pushing a broom or stocking shelves from nine to five. Sometimes, almost as a lark, some of these young men will work for a few days or a few weeks at some special job, perhaps one funded by a branch of government to "cool off the cities." An example of this kind of job was to go around putting large chalked X's on neighborhood garbage cans to warn the building owner that the receptacle was defective and in violation of sanitation ordinances. These jobs were seen as simple, undemanding ways to hustle a little money, entertain oneself and one's neighbors, and thumb a nose at the absentee landlords. Such work is also to be forgotten as soon as possible.

Although the unemployment rate for teenagers and young adults has always been high, sometimes reaching disastrous proportions, it seems possible that some part of this may now be voluntary. The negative attitude toward the kind of work described above is known and talked about by the young people in the context of the changed view of themselves held by Young Blacks who grew up during the civil rights movement and the Black Power years of ethnic assertiveness. These young people talk more about not accepting Whitey's views of work and their expected low-status, low-pay place in the economic system. They especially contrast themselves with the older people, who are more likely to be *under*employed or seriously disturbed by their inability to secure and hold a job.

Yet obviously others, often these same older people, especially those with families, do take on work that is dead-end and minimally paid, such as domestic day work, dishwashing and other restaurant-trades work, stockroom work, elevator operating, and janitorial and security jobs. These are the people who earn less than $100 a week.

Most households in Blackston that are supported primarily by wages include two or more individuals who work. A typical pattern is a husband who works at a trade like truck driving, a wife who is in domestic service or factory work, and one or two teenage children who may have part-time service jobs, such as waitressing or clerking. Particularly if the household is a large one and includes a good many young children or unemployed adult kin who take care of the house and children, even these joint incomes are far from sufficient. Such a family usually remains chronically in debt. If they attempt to live up to goals such as house ownership, and many do, any minor change in their wage picture, such as the loss of employment for just one member of the unit, often means the loss of property in which they have invested considerable funds and great effort.

WELFARE. The term "welfare" is used here to mean all forms of public assistance, including home relief, payments to the blind and disabled, social security, unemployment compensation, and stipends paid to women with young children. The payment level of any of these forms of assistance is inadequate for survival. But because the law prohibits recipients of these forms of assistance from having most other forms of income while receiving welfare payments, almost every person in Blackston who receives some form of welfare payment is forced to break the law to survive.

At the time of the study, welfare or public assistance, particularly that paid to women with children, allowed approximately $200 a month, excluding rent, to a family of four, or a yearly total of almost $2,500—less than half the amount required for the government's own "low" standard-of-living estimate. Despite the limited contribution of welfare to individuals and family/kin units, it serves as an important basic source of income for many Blackstonians. Welfare survival meant using about $1.60 per person per day to pay for all costs of food, clothing, personal incidentals, school expenses, entertainment, transportation, fuel for heating and cooking, electric service, and sales tax.

Welfare payment levels in Blackston may seem high to residents of other states partly because they are unaware of the distinction between welfare recipients and welfare beneficiaries. Consider that the average rental for a very rundown four-room apartment during the period of study was about $150, with some rents as high as $250 or more a month. The vast majority of tenement housing is owned by White noncommunity people. The welfare department sets no upper limit on the amount it will pay to the landlord, nor does it require or enforce any minimum housing standards or conditions of upkeep. In some cases the money is sent directly to the landlord by the welfare department and is never even seen by the tenant. Thus the system provides substantial subsidies to landlord-beneficiaries.

Because of the housing shortage in the city in general and the discrimination against ethnic minorities and welfare recipients in particular, frequently as much as 40 percent of a family's total welfare grant goes into rent. The Bureau of Labor Statistics worker's family budget allocates less than 20 percent for housing in most cities, and the median national figure for housing costs as a percentage of income is under 15 percent. But no matter what amount the landlord receives, the person defined as "on welfare" has only $1.60 per day to spend for all living expenses except rent.

Food is the other major item to which all Blackstonians, whether on welfare or not, must devote a large proportion of their income. Often the people of Blackston must pay more for the same items than residents of Euro-American districts in the same city (see David Caplovitz, *The Poor Pay More*, 1963). Our own work in Blackston included a survey of prevailing prices for twenty-five basic and popular items, including milk, rice, chicken, and collard greens, in three kinds of stores. These were three small, independent neighborhood stores, three supermarkets within the community, and three supermarkets in predominantly non-Black, middle-class areas within a mile or two of Blackston. Two of the outside supermarkets were parts of the same chain as two of the Blackston supermarkets.

The following chart shows the results of this survey with the in-community (small independents and supermarkets) prices lumped together to highlight the contrast across community lines. Within Blackston it is true that supermarket prices are somewhat lower than neighborhood grocery prices, but these differences were neither so great nor so consistent as those between communities.

Welfare recipients, whose food budget is sharply limited, are aware of these patterns, and most will go to a great deal of effort

COMMERCIAL RETAIL PRICES, 1969

PRODUCT	AVERAGE PRICE IN WHITE AREAS	AVERAGE PRICE IN BLACKSTON	DIFFERENCE BETWEEN PRICES
Meat & eggs			
Stew beef	92¢ lb.	94¢ lb.	+ 2%
Pork ribs	89¢ lb.	93¢ lb.	+ 4
Chicken	39¢ lb.	53¢ lb.	+ 36
Neck bones	31¢ lb.	36¢ lb.	+ 16
Medium eggs	75¢ doz.	84¢ doz.	+ 12
Dairy & bakery products			
Whole milk	32¢ qt.	30¢ qt.	− 6
White bread	33¢ loaf	33¢ loaf	0
Vegetables			
Collards (frozen)	18¢ pkg.	25¢ pkg.	+ 39
String beans (frozen)	22¢ pkg.	25¢ pkg.	+ 14
Broccoli (frozen)	28¢ pkg.	39¢ pkg.	+ 39
Rice	26¢ lb.	42¢ lb.	+ 62
Tomatoes	30¢ pkg.	33¢ pkg.	+ 10
Fruit			
Oranges	5¢ ea.	8¢ ea.	+ 60
Apples	14¢ lb.	25¢ lb.	+ 79
Bananas	15¢ lb.	16¢ lb.	+ 7
Beverages			
Beer	$1.26 6-pack	$1.33 6-pack	+ 6
Soda	$ .95 6-pack	$1.00 6-pack	+ 5
Nonfood items			
Detergent	28¢ lb.	37¢ lb.	+ 32
Bath soap	11¢ cake	14¢ cake	+ 27
Toilet paper	14¢ roll	15¢ roll	+ 7
		AVERAGE DIFFERENCE	+ 23%

and expense to shop in a more favorable area. This, rather than laziness or extravagance, accounts for the wide use of service cars on welfare-check day. Welfare mothers not only know that prices on such items as rice and chicken are appreciably lower outside of the Blackston community; they also want the higher-quality merchandise and greater variety in brands and packaged quantities that are available outside Blackston. Spoiled meat, wilted vegetables, and sour milk are common in Blackston, rare in nearby middle-class areas.

Caught between the very limited food budgets available through welfare grants and the obvious advantages of shopping outside the community, many men and women from Blackston will brave the coolness or outright hostility of shopkeepers and regular customers in other communities and the demands of time, distance, and transportation costs to make a welfare food budget as effective as possible.

HUSTLING. "Hustling," both in Blackston and in this book, refers to a wide variety of unconventional, sometimes extralegal or illegal activities, often frowned upon by the wider community but widely accepted and practiced in the slums and ghettos of large cities. As sources of income, the benefits from hustling are sometimes more anticipated than real, as with all activities involving chance. Yet everyone beyond early childhood has knowledge of and at least indirect contact with these operations, often only as customers or extremely peripheral workers.

An example of hustling is the "numbers game," or "policy," where one may make a bet ranging from ten cents up to hundreds of dollars each day in an attempt to predict a three-digit number. The winning number is often based on a figure available daily and theoretically not subject to manipulation, such as the last three digits of all monies bet each day at a particular race track on a particular race. This number is published in daily newspapers and is available for bettors to check. Although betting on the numbers is illegal, the amount wagered every day by Blackstonians was enormous. On Paul Street alone there were often three or four people who daily wrote down each bet of friends and neighbors, collected money, recorded the material, and passed these on to the next level in a highly organized network. These same numbers writers are responsible for distributing the payoff money when a player correctly predicts, or "hits," the number. Numbers writers are very low-level workers and often are paid only a small commission on the bets they take. Sometimes they receive a share of the winnings or a gift if one of their customers hits. In turn, it is the street-level writers or collectors who are most often subject to arrest rather than those at higher levels, who "bank" tens of thousands of dollars each day.

People in Blackston also hustle by buying and selling "hot" goods, whose source is often unknown but correctly assumed to be stolen or otherwise illegally obtained; gambling (most often card games, pool or billiards, craps); bootlegging liquor after hours or on Sunday; stealing cars and/or stripping them of salable parts; stripping abandoned buildings of salable parts such as copper tubing and fixtures; shoplifting; looting; highjacking; running con games; and trafficking in narcotics. This list is not meant to be exhaustive. For example, some individuals might include such clearly illegal activities as mugging, burglary, or even armed robbery under the heading of hustling while many Blackstonians would reserve the term for activities that are more widespread, or merely strongly disapproved and less violent.

In his autobiography, Malcolm X describes the place of hustling in a particular Black community that he knew well: "Everyone in Harlem needed some kind of hustle to survive, and needed to stay high in some way to forget what they had to *do* to survive."

In Blackston many residents are willing, open, and active participants and beneficiaries of such activities as gambling ("the numbers") and buying and selling stolen merchandise, particularly food, clothing, and jewelry. Other Blackstonians are both victims and minor profiteers of drug activity, such as the buying and selling of marijuana, methadone, cocaine, and heroin. Some Blackston people are also unwilling victims of mugging and burglary.

Because burglary often involves knowing whether a particular home has worthwhile possessions as well as knowing something about the habits of the intended victims (for example, when the man is at work, whether the woman has taken the children out, whether some other member of the household has been left in the apartment or house), successful burglaries without violence are most often committed by one's own neighbors, who have an excuse for being in the area and knowing these things. Such factors work against the ideal sometimes expressed by burglars among our acquaintance, who say they try not to rob on the same street or within several blocks of where they live. After talking with Blackstonians who admit to having mugged someone and with Blackstonians who have been victims of muggers, I believe that muggers rarely do mug within their immediate neighborhood.

Despite the variety of specific behaviors accepted, acted on, or implied by the term "hustling," there is general agreement that hustling is meant to produce some benefit or gain from activity that is less structured and less time-limited than conventional nine-to-five employment. Or, as many Blackston residents, as well as Black people more widely, say, "I did what I had to do to survive. Black people know how to survive."

Because of the illegal and often unpredictable nature of most hustling, it is difficult to determine precisely what proportion of anyone's income is provided through hustling. But it is clear that most of the population of Blackston takes part in such activities at some time, to some degree, and to some benefit.

THE PEOPLE

THE THREE GROUPS of people described in the following pages are typical of Blackston residents in a number of ways. First, they all include related persons who often are spread over a number of households. Such households may be located in other parts of the city or state or in different states. Members of such families, particularly children, frequently move from one household to another. Adult members of each household expect to receive mutual aid from one another in the form of money, food, child care, and other physical and emotional support. Second, each of the families covers a broad age range, usually from infants or small children to grandparents or great-grandparents. Third, each of these families shows the range of economic adaptations and behavior styles represented by welfare, hustling, and other hard work. Often there is a variety of styles within a single household. Sometimes these differences can be seen by comparing one member of the family with another. Sometimes a single individual may change over a period of time from a reliance on hustling to a reliance on employment or welfare or some other ordering of sources of income.

All the families and individuals described here are real people whose names have been changed to protect their privacy: these are not ideal types or composites. All the activities described here really happened. In a few cases, where a specific action would identify an individual and that individual has protested, I have substituted a comparable but more disguised incident. Many of the activities described occurred in my presence. Where this is the case that fact is included as part of the text. There are instances in which the presence of two anthropologists also helps to illustrate the kinds of interactions that went on between us and other Blackstonians on a daily basis for five years. Activities not directly seen by the researchers have been, where possible, substantiated by several other persons. The thoughts attributed to the characters were expressed by those persons in a number of situations. Much of the material is available in tape recordings or in field notes. In the three stories some of the action has been telescoped in order to tell a story more clearly. I do not believe that this in any way invalidates the data.

The people described in these pages have a variety of backgrounds and current responses to life. There are grade-school dropouts, high-school graduates, and one person with some college training. Some of these people have conventional jobs at which they have worked for decades; some do not. Sometimes they go to church; more often they do not. Sometimes they help their children with school homework; sometimes they do not. Sometimes they help in block cleanup campaigns; sometimes they do not. Some belong to labor unions; some do not. Sometimes they vote; sometimes they don't.

Because the people described here are real and do display the variety, mixture, and change in income source and life styles seen in Blackston, their lives seem to me to support the view that there is no hard-and-fast difference within Blackston between people who could be described as culturally ghetto people and others who are only circumstantially in the ghetto. There are two features these people have in common that affect them importantly despite the many different ways in which they act and react to their situation: Blackstonians are Black and poor in a rich, White, racist society.

Hustling: The Burtons RANDY- ADDICT/DEALER

IT WASN'T EVEN NOON yet and Randy was already tired. The physical labor of knocking out the brass and copper plumbing fixtures in this abandoned house was only part of the reason for feeling tired. After all, he had been up since before dawn helping the two families up the street move what was salvageable from the still smoldering ruins of Hank's house. Randy knew that fires were common occurrences in his neighborhood, though he didn't know that statistically the area had the highest fire rate in the city. But he agreed with Hank that a house that had had three fires in less than a year must be especially cursed. Just that morning Hank had vowed never to live in that house again even though he "owned" it, as he often liked to tell people. Only if Randy or some other neighbor was especially angry with Hank would he point out that Hank wouldn't own the house for at least twenty years and the house probably wouldn't last that long.

Randy wasn't angry with Hank today. Hank had given Randy and Jim B. $10 each for helping to move clothes, some furniture, and small items, most of them scorched or waterlogged, into the basement of Hank's sister's house, just three doors away. Hank could afford to spend the money because he had forced his way back into the burned house in time to stop the firemen from going through the bedroom dresser drawers, where his money was cached. Besides, as Randy and every other addict on the street was aware, whatever it cost in cash to salvage items from a burned house was cheaper than losing everything to the people who would certainly go through the abandoned building later that day or night, looking for anything usable or salable. While Randy was carting things under Hank's direction, he had already noticed some potentially worthwhile items that Hank wasn't saving. Others, especially children and teenagers, would have fun just rummaging through the debris that had been scattered by ax-wielding firemen.

Any change in the day's routine was welcomed by the younger people. A dozen kids were already working hard to help the upstairs family move their goods into a neighbor's basement. The boys knew they probably wouldn't be paid, so they did it for fun, praise, and only the tiniest hope of getting some spending money.

Part of Randy's $10 had already gone for cigarettes and a bottle of Twist. He smoked unfiltered Pall Malls, called jailhouse cigarettes because they were the single brand distributed in the city's jails. Randy had an addict's dislike for hard liquor, but Twist or Thunderbird wine was nice to keep a high going and to smooth off the edges of the rough world. Normally he and Jim B. would have had their own version of an ongoing argument about the relative merits of Twist versus Thunderbird, and the issue would be decided by whoever had contributed most to the collection of quarters, dimes, and pennies that the two of them and two or three other momentarily idle men would have put together. Today Randy bought his own favorite. And today he wasn't idle either.

Early this morning he had helped Hank after the fire. This afternoon he had found an abandoned house farther down the street. He spent the afternoon in the basement of this abandoned house stripping it of plumbing fixtures. After scraping each pipe or fixture to determine which was copper and which brass, he had to dismantle the valuable items with the crudest of tools and cart the pieces to a safe place. A safe place meant one from which they wouldn't be stolen by someone else until he arranged to transport them to the junk dealer, who paid 26¢ a pound for scrap metal. The junk dealer was one of the few Whites who still lived in Blackston. He never asked where the fixtures came from or why he had so many repeat customers.

Randy, who had dropped out of school in sixth grade, about a dozen years ago, would probably fail any standard mathematics test. Yet he was perfect at figuring out quickly the income from any size load of brass and how to divide up the amount earned among the people who had helped him scavenge or transport. He was as accurate but not always as responsible about the much larger sums of money that sometimes came his way.

It was only two weeks ago that the very people he was helping this morning had helped to rescue him when the drug dealer had sent three men armed with a gun, a baseball bat, and a metal bar to get Randy. Randy's young wife, Darla, had left their three children in the apartment, with Randy barricaded in the tiny windowless bathroom, while she ran across to Hank's house and used the phone to call the police. The sincerity of Darla's hysteria and her mention of the gun seemed enough to get the police to act very quickly. In this neighborhood crimes often were completed and the guilty parties long gone before the police arrived. Sometimes it seemed to speed up police response if you said that a White person was being threatened or was somehow involved. Fortunately for Randy, the police responded immediately this time with several cars and armed officers, who arrived on the street with weapons drawn.

Children in Blackston learn early to dash for their own homes, stoops, or doorways whenever there is a hassle on the street. They did so on this occasion, and the police were able to catch the three men who had threatened Randy just as one threw his gun under an automobile at the curb. The men were arrested and carted away. Randy came out of hiding and went to the police station too. He was safe for the moment, but he knew that if he ever pressed charges against the men he wouldn't remain safe. Besides, he had no interest in pressing charges. This time he had won. He had sold some of the man's dope and kept all of the man's money, and the dealer had learned never again to trust Randy. Drug dealing, especially at the street level, was always a balance between the need to trust others—your supplier, your customers, the cop you were paying off—and the knowledge that no one could be trusted. So the dealer had taken a chance and lost. Had his men caught Randy they would have tried to get the man's money, they would certainly have beaten Randy unmercifully, and possibly killed him. But now the three would-be attackers had a different problem, and the dealer had much more lucrative work to do in this area, where so many young men and women were using heroin. He wouldn't waste any more time or effort on Randy.

For Randy, who lived from day to day with no steady source of income, it would be better if his activities were successful in obtaining money without the contributors' being aware of it. Some of his hustles had been smooth. For instance, he and Coleman had worked on this very street and several others close by on a project that didn't require the hard physical labor of his present copper and brass gathering. All the earlier hustle had required were some clean, neat clothes and a smooth line about collecting contributions so that a local pentecostal church could help with the funeral expenses of some children recently killed in a fire on a street only two or three blocks away. Such a story was easily accepted because it was common knowledge that fires happened often in this area, welfare funeral payments were inadequate for anything except a pauper's wooden box, and churches and neighbors often contributed in such a situation. With these things in their favor and with their own respectful presentation, almost no one would suspect that these were addicts hustling for their fix, drink, and food.

Randy and almost all his friends and fellow addicts felt very strongly about personal cleanliness. Most were young married men or young adults living with their parents. Their clothing would fluctuate greatly in quantity and quality depending upon the money available above and beyond the cost of drugs. Clothes were sent to the cleaners often, even though the redemption date might be postponed for weeks or months. Other items would be subject to rigorous, heavily bleached washing by the females of the family. In Blackston the image of the dirty, smelly, ill-kempt addict seems largely a TV creation and more often the exception than the rule.

Randy thought back on a recent amusing experience. A British TV team had chosen the building in which he lived as the locale for a documentary about poverty in Blackston. Anyone on Paul Street could have told them—but no one did—that of all the other possibilities they had chosen a six-family tenement in which four of the families had active addict members. In this case, Randy's amusement came from knowing something about the community that was known by neither the news team nor the local poverty-program official who guided the news team. Not everyone was amused. Some people on the street were unhappy that their community should be represented by "those people," and some people were jealous of the attention.

Everyone on the street was aware of who the addicts were, where they lived, their parents, their spouses, and their children. Everyone on the street was somewhat more careful of his personal possessions when an addict was around, and some people refused to allow an addict into their house or apartment under any circumstances, but in general most of the people reacted to and interacted with addicts and their families on the basis of the same personal characteristics and kin ties that operated in other cases.

Randy knew he had lots of friends. Though many people may have suspected that he was responsible for some of their own losses through housebreaking or pilfering, Randy was careful on Paul Street, and most of his money-raising activities took place in the surrounding community. Besides, when materials from the railroad cars that were stored on the siding one block east became available—plastic bowls, toys, or sacks of potatoes or onions—Randy would sell them at very low prices to his friends and neighbors. He was also generous with money when he had more than enough to meet his immediate needs. He would buy wine freely, lend money to a wide range of buddies, and give quarters to many of the children on the street, who immediately bought soda, candy, or potato chips.

Randy climbed out of the basement of this two-family house that had been abandoned just a few days earlier by a Black family and a Spanish family who could neither find the landlord and demand basic repairs nor pay for the upkeep of a rapidly deteriorating and hard-to-heat house. He saw the young wife and mother who had been burned out just this morning. It would be fun to "rap" with her—he might even talk her into bed sometime—but right now it was more important to see if she would be willing to move the brass and copper in her car. He knew that she wanted to study the community and was willing to be useful and go anywhere to do this, so he thought his chances for getting help were good. Besides, he had just moved some of her things to a neighbor's basement after the fire this morning. And if Miz Valentine would take him up to the junk dealer, he'd offer to buy gas and maybe talk her into taking him over to the open-air market too. He sure needed to buy some blue jeans with the money he was about to earn.

She agreed, and Randy loaded the pipes, joints, and fixtures into the car. This woman didn't look different from so many of the females in the community, who were strong and healthy though inclined to be overweight because of the local diet, rich in rice, beans, and various kinds of pork fat. The fact that she didn't help Randy load the car was related to community standards about the division of labor and work roles between the sexes, not to her health or strength. Although a woman might move a refrigerator in the process of cleaning house, she was not expected to lift items that might be lighter but were defined as male work. The young men on the street—addicts, older men, and youngsters—invariably offered to carry and sometimes insisted on carrying groceries in from the car for female kin, friends, or just neighbors. When the same women lifted and moved heavy garbage cans in order to sweep the sidewalk in front of their house, none of these same males would interrupt their nodding, rapping, or playing activities to help. Men and boys of all ages worked on cars and stripped parts from stolen vehicles brought to

Paul Street or the block of empty lots beside the railroad tracks. Sometimes a small girl would join the other youngsters in bouncing about on the seats of such cars, but even at the age of four or five the girls were aware that stripping and repairing cars were strictly male activities.

As Randy and his young female friend drove to the junkyard, he thought about housework. One of his few steady sources of small change was the weekly mopping that "Aunt" Bea paid him to do in the hallways of the two tenements next to his own. He didn't consider this woman's work. He also mopped the floors for Darla, especially if she was unhappy about his recent behavior toward the house or the children or her. He had even heard Hank bragging that he could clean the house faster than his wife, Bernice. He had also sat around on a Saturday drinking with them while they both cooked, cleaned, and socialized with relatives and friends. Maybe men were more free to define what was acceptable for themselves. Some of those "young jive turkeys" just starting to stay out of school and hang around on the block were afraid to be seen with a broom, but they'd learn you had to do anything to survive. Randy had learned this on the street and in the man's joint while locked up too.

Randy brought himself out of these thoughts as the car pulled up in front of the junk dealer's. His driver had never been here, but she recognized the place when Randy described it as one block down from the new methadone center. For one thing, several people had been mugged and a woman had been killed recently nearby. Of course, everyone blamed it on the addicts, but Randy wasn't convinced. As he saw it, an addict wasn't money-hungry, especially if he had a fix. An addict just wanted not to be bothered. All those guys at the methadone center were getting a free fix every day—in exchange for a urine sample to make sure they weren't using heroin too. It certainly cut down on street crime. It was even noticeable on Paul Street. The number of housebreakings had gone down. That was what the authorities were interested in, as Randy saw it—cutting down crime. That was how they sold the methadone program, especially in the ghetto.

But then again, some of his old buddies were getting methadone, and it seemed to make them crazy. For instance, the people on methadone drank a lot. A good heroin high didn't make you want to get drunk or act wild. Randy wanted nothing to do with methadone. He and Jim B. and Jack had discussed it many a night. They all agreed that methadone didn't make you any less an addict, it just hung you up on a different drug, one that was even harder to quit. Jack had been a sometime addict for the past twenty-five years. He had quit heroin many times, either because he was in jail or in a hospital, or because the stuff wasn't available, or even because he decided to straighten up and go to work. But he was aware that the saying "once an addict, always an addict" was true and his case was classic. Randy liked Jack. In fact, after Jim B. Jack was his main man. He might just buy some barbecue for himself and Jack tonight. They could go to his place, since Darla had the kids and was visiting her mother in another part of town. And Jack probably didn't have anyplace to stay tonight. He had been living on that old couch in Hank's basement but was burned out as of this morning.

Coming back to the moment, Randy figured he'd better keep his eye on this man while the brass and copper were being weighed or he wouldn't have any money to spend tonight. Randy finished the deal and then insisted on buying gas for the car, even pointing out to Miz Valentine that the money would have gone to a service-car driver if he could have found one willing to transport the pipes, but the anthropologist refused to accept any payment. Randy figured that perhaps he ought to rap a little more to this sweet girl and try to get her instead of Jack to keep him company tonight. After all, he could get together with Jack anytime, and he had been trying for months to make out with her. She had lived on Paul Street for years, but only recently had Randy started to really talk to her and tease her, after he noticed that her husband didn't seem as uptight about such behavior as some of the men on the street.

She refused to spend any more time with Randy and instead insisted that he hurry and buy what he needed at the market so that she could join her husband and son at the friend's house where they had been taken in after the fire. Randy was momentarily disappointed, but sex was not a major interest of his. He knew that this relative lack of sex drive was an effect of the dope. He also knew that if he once got aroused, he was good for hours, and he tried with a combination of joking and delicacy to convey this to the young lady. He knew his rap was good, but she wasn't having any. Randy had never heard of anyone else making out with her either, but something convinced him that he could. Randy thought of himself as attractive and knew that he had been successful in seducing other females, even here on Paul Street, where he lived with his wife and three small children.

Randy had lived on Paul Street for a long time. Earlier he had lived with his father, his twin brother, an older brother who still lived on Paul Street, and one sister. Then the family had moved from Blackston to another part of the city. After he had married Darla, when they were both sixteen and had their first child, he moved back into the very building where he had lived before with his father. His father had since moved a dozen blocks farther east and was living with Johneva, his only daughter, and her three sons. Right now Johneva was off drugs, and only took the tranquilizers prescribed for her by the hospital. She was doing a good job of caring for the children and the apartment while her father worked. Randy was happy for this development, since Johneva was his favorite sibling. She was smart and had a lot of common sense and a caustic tongue.

Johneva, the oldest of the Burton children, was especially fond of Randy too. She even liked Randy's wife, though she didn't think Darla was too bright. The two women had not been at all friendly for a long time after Darla had thrown hot grease on Randy during a family fight. But Randy had healed well. The doctors had fixed his face so that no scar showed, and if he chose to stay with Darla that was his business. Besides, even Johneva admitted that Randy had been irresponsible toward his own child when Darla left him to babysit. But then again, Darla also knew that Randy had been on heroin since before they were married, and she should have known not to expect him to be responsible when he was nodding.

Johneva philosophized that one lived with these things, let bygones be bygones, and tried to survive. She became friendly again with Darla and occasionally brought her sons over to Darla's house to play with their cousins. Bobby was now seven and Carolee four. Randy's third child, Maury, was just a few weeks old.

Being married and having children didn't interfere with Randy's attractiveness in the eyes of other females, and heroin reduced but didn't destroy his extramarital sexual activities. Randy, like most other young males, spent more time rapping to women and bragging to his male friends than he spent in doing what he promised or claimed. He assumed that everyone else exaggerated as much as he did. One good thing about all the talking was that one could slip in the name of someone with whom one had really been intimate among a number of names that everyone would assume were fantasy and wishful thinking or bragging. Randy had no desire to get any girl, or himself, into trouble.

Here in Blackston a small number of couples, particularly older people, seemed to be faithful to each other for religious or moral reasons. A few seemed so inclined for personal reasons, but most people in the community who voiced any opinion seemed to expect or at least not to be surprised at extramarital activity. Behavior both preceded and flowed from opinion. One would be more strongly criticized for not being discreet than for the basic sexual behavior. It was generally agreed, and Randy shared the belief, that what was really offensive was to conduct yourself so that other people would be forced to be aware of your behavior and would communicate this awareness to your spouse. "Don't do it in my face" was often the overt message delivered by a wronged spouse in a public confrontation.

For example, Randy knew and even expected that Darla would have a male consort while Randy served time in "the joint." But it was done quietly, and the affair ended when Randy came back from jail. Many of the people on the street were aware of Darla's consort and not particularly critical. Darla provided a secure base, cooked, washed, cared for the children, and did all the things she would otherwise be doing for Randy, while the young consort provided sexual companionship, helped shop, helped care for the children, and had a place from which to carry on his own hustles.

The hustle that had landed Randy in the joint on this occasion involved an attempt to move up the ladder in the dope hierarchy, just one step from consumer to distributor, with about a dozen addicts working for him. This was made possible by joining with Jim B. and Sly, who had recently earned some money through a policy game "hit." With the money they bought cocaine in the adjoining White residential area and planned to sell it in Blackston. The White distributor didn't want to be made conspicuous by having a lot of Black people knocking at his door, so he was willing to sell a large amount of coke for a good deal less than it would eventually bring and let these Black men worry about selling it in the Black community. While serving his time in jail, Randy came to think that he, Jim B., and Sly had been naive to believe they could move up without making the necessary payments for protection.

When the police busted into the Blackston apartment where the three men had the remainder of undistributed, unsold cocaine and some of the cash from the day's sales, Randy agreed to "take the weight," or confess, and exonerate Jim B. and Sly. This was not something that had been worked out. Even Randy would find it hard to explain why he chose to take the blame. Fortunately, his old lady, Darla, was already holding some of the money. And at that moment it seemed reasonable for only one person to go to jail, especially since the cops weren't really interested in them but wanted a lead to someone higher up. All three men refused to "give up somebody" or name their supplier, out of fear of the consequences to their own continued supply, their reputation in drug circles, and their physical safety, and because of the widely accepted view that to be a rat, or informer, was morally worse than to be a drug addict.

This ended Randy's three-year run of time in the street without getting busted. He had obviously been luckier than his young friend Gary, who had yet to make one solid year's run. The only other time Randy had spent in the joint was at the age of nineteen, when he was in and out of army stockades. He had been a full-blown practicing addict with marks up and down his arms when he was drafted. Darla sent him drugs while he was stationed in the Southwest. But even high on heroin Randy hadn't liked the army, so he would go AWOL, return to Blackston, and neither hide nor resist arrest when it came. After he got out of the army he hung his dishonorable-discharge paper over the single bunk bed in the sparsely furnished apartment he shared with Darla.

Randy came back from all these rambling thoughts and

wondered if his recent talks with the anthropologists who lived and worked on Paul Street were responsible for the sudden increase in reminiscing. He had always disliked the question, "What are you thinking?," but he found that he enjoyed talking into the anthropologists' tape recorder. It was not that he always knew what to say. Just yesterday he had made the point that he couldn't explain why he was a junkie. He remembered going on to say, "If any man tells you he can explain, he's lying." Randy didn't mind going into great descriptive detail about the drug scene, but he definitely didn't want to think about why he was a part of it.

Randy remembered being off heroin for months at a time—while he was in the stockade, most of the year he was in the joint later, and once while he was on the street. That last time there just wasn't any heroin on the street. He'd been pretty damn sick and miserable for a while, but he knew that fear of physical withdrawal wasn't what kept him on the stuff. Each time he had gone back to heroin when it became available.

Well, here he was back on Paul Street. He tried again to pay his driver and even took time for a lighthearted cursory "rap," but she was obviously worried about other things and drove off quickly. It was time to go find Jack and get them both something to eat and a bag or two of dope. It had been a good day—but there was no telling what tomorrow would bring.

THIS WAS DARLA's second day back after visiting her mother. She had to get used to her own house again after being in a place that had so much furniture and so many items that weren't basic necessities. Her own house and those of most of her closest friends—Jim B.'s wife, Belvie, and Ann—had only beds, a kitchen table and chairs, and one or two living-room pieces. For the last few months she'd had a not-so-good TV set that Randy had brought home. She had insisted on keeping it, though she knew that if things got really tight and Randy needed a fix he might try to sell it. Her mother's house had so many nice things: kitchen items like a toaster, matched pots and pans, and a blender. She also had a new bedroom suite she was still paying on, a hi-fi, and a color TV. Darla enjoyed these things when she visited, but she didn't ever expect to have them herself, and she was used to what she did have. The real reason she enjoyed visiting her mother, to whom she had always been close, was that she could talk to her and get good advice. The two of them sat around for two days, cooked only when they felt like it, sent the children to play with an upstairs neighbor's children, smoked some marijuana, and talked about all the people they knew. Darla's mother had known Randy since he was a young child and had always liked him. It was good to talk to her about Randy, describing some of his unpredictable activities and their own life together. Although her mother didn't approve, she was the only one who had understood Darla's side of things when Randy was in the hospital with the hot-grease burns.

Darla was back home and up early today because she had agreed to let that anthropologist spend the day at her house watching what the children ate. The woman had said she was doing some kind of study of the food eaten by babies and children in Blackston. Darla wasn't sure why she had agreed. She thought Randy had been paying too much attention to this anthropologist lately, and she couldn't imagine what he saw in that light-skinned old woman. Darla had very mixed feelings about that woman. There she was, married to a White man, and with all that education of hers she didn't even sound Black. Still, both the anthropologists had lived here in Blackston for over three years and so they weren't the same as the White landlord next door who came around once a month on rent day. The woman had always been friendly to her, had taken the children to the emergency room once when the ambulance didn't come, and had helped when those people tried to shoot Randy. Doing favors for people who did favors for you was an important part of getting along.

Besides, like many people in Blackston, Darla's anti-White feeling was not an active force that inspired aggressive action. For example, Darla would never try to prevent any White person from living here on Paul Street, like those White people did to the Paul Street family who tried to move into a single-family house a few miles away. The White neighbors-to-be burned the newly bought house to the ground. In another neighboring White area they had closed down the elementary school for weeks because twenty children from Blackston were to be bused to the school.

Well, anyway she had agreed and it was just as easy to go ahead and spend the day with Miz Valentine. She certainly didn't plan to do anything special.

Miz Valentine arrived and took a seat at the kitchen table. Darla went on with her activities. After Bobby was washed, dressed, fed, and sent to school with Belvie's two older girls, Darla cooked up some grits for herself, Carolee, and the baby, did the dishes, and turned on the TV. Maybe Miz Valentine would suggest getting a little something to drink, since she always seemed to have a little money. Darla had no money and hadn't had any for several days now. She couldn't go shopping even though she needed things. It was still almost three days till the welfare check was due, and she had already used up the food stamps too. With less than $2 a day for herself and each of the children, all the welfare check went for clothes for the children and food for the family. She hadn't bought anything for herself for months. Bobby was almost seven and needed nice clothes to wear to school. He was getting wilder too and wearing out shoes and pants so fast.

Sometimes Randy brought home some money or some item they could use and wouldn't have to buy, but she never knew when this was going to happen. At Easter she had made such a fuss that Randy had gotten himself together and come up with some money from somewhere. Often she asked how he got the money and other times she didn't want to know. You couldn't always trust Randy's answers either. What was important was that the children had looked beautiful. Darla was proud that they were dressed as well as anyone on the street. Even her mother had been impressed when she saw the Easter Day pictures of the children taken by the woman sitting right here. Bobby had a suit, new shoes, a trench coat, and a cap. Carolee looked darling in white lace tights, white shoes and hat, a new dress, and a blue cape with white trim. All in all the pictures were beautiful. The day had been a good one. No one went anywhere except for a few people who went to church, but everyone visited from house to house and paraded up and down the street.

When Darla got tired of answering questions about her relatives, when and where they were born and all that other stuff Miz Valentine used in making what she called a kinship chart, she left the lady in the house with the baby and went next door to get Belvie to come sit with them and watch the late-morning TV programs. Darla and Belvie had been watching these for years, in one house or another. They knew all the characters, remembered their changes over the years, and often argued about whether one person or another in a given series had done the right thing or discussed what they themselves would do in the same situation. They both agreed that the women on these shows knew what life was about. And lately there was even a Black person in some of the shows.

What Darla really needed to talk to Belvie about was the possibility that "Uncle" Jonesy, who lived directly across the street from Darla, might be getting a large shipment of grass and would want them to help him package it and sell it. Just as it was respectful to call all adult women, no matter what their marital status, "Miz" and adult men "Mister," it was a sign of both respect and affection to give some of the more outgoing and community-involved people like Bea and Jonesy the titles "aunt" and "uncle."

Selling marijuana was one of the ways in which Darla was able to earn money to spend on herself if she wanted to. Besides, she enjoyed smoking it—the world sort of floated by, people were nicer, things were funnier, food tasted better, and you felt relaxed. It wasn't a bad way to earn money, and it hurt no one. You could do it anytime, you didn't have to leave your house if you didn't want to, and customers often shared some of what they bought with you.

Darla occasionally thought about other possible work, some way to get enough money for some sharp shoes or clothes or to be able to go to a movie or a dance. She didn't even have as much money to spend as those young girls down the street who worked for the summer youth program. There wasn't anything of that sort just a few years earlier when she had been a teenager. If there had been, she would have joined. Those kids didn't even work, and after the first few days they didn't even have to stay at the headquarters. Dulcie had told her they just went up to the headquarters, signed in, and left again. They were supposed to be taught to do office work or work in the community, but only a few of the boys were sent out to help clean up streets and empty lots. The rest of them drifted back down and hung out on Dulcie's porch. Then at the end of the week they'd get a check. They certainly didn't learn to work. Darla and Belvie watched the teenage males and females all hang out and predicted that Dulcie would be pregnant by the end of the summer. In the meantime they were getting a little money from this summer program, and Darla knew she could count on them to buy some of the grass she and Belvie would soon have.

Darla sometimes even considered getting a job like the one her mother had as an aide in a hospital. Belvie had gone down and applied last week. Belvie's youngest, Johnnie, was eight now, and the two girls, especially Darlene, who was almost twelve, could take care of the house by themselves. Belvie said that going to the hospital had been a waste of time. You just had to walk in the back door and listen to the voices of the aides and service workers and it was clear that "only West Indians need apply." Darla's mother, who had begun work at the county hospital shortly after her husband had been killed almost fifteen years ago, had been telling her just recently that the county hospital as well as private hospitals seemed to hire only West Indians nowadays. Those West Indians stuck close together and got each other jobs as soon as they heard about them. As soon as the hospitals had to hire lots of Black people so that they would look good after all the civil rights business, and when the neighborhood around them had changed, they began using lots of West Indians. Everyone, the West Indians themselves, the store owners over on the avenue who hired them as clerks, the personnel people in hospitals and department stores, seemed to think that West Indians were a step above plain Black people. Some people liked those accents. Some people said that West Indians had more schooling and worked harder. Maybe so, since you had to have more schooling to get into this country, and you sure had to work hard in those shitty jobs. In fact, Darla knew she didn't want to stand up all day or be around sick people too much. She didn't even want to work for the phone company like her sister-in-law did. They didn't pay much, and they sure were hard to work for.

There was her sister-in-law going to work every day, leaving her children with her mother, Miz Jay. As Darla saw it, Renée didn't have much to show for all this except a few more clothes that she had to have to wear to work. Otherwise Renée lived on the same street, in the same kind of house, ate the same food, went to the same parties. She probably didn't even have as much fun, since she didn't drink or smoke and she hardly had time to spend with her children and friends. Darla would much rather hustle grass sometimes than work eight to five all the time.

Darla and Belvie stopped over at Bernice's for a few minutes and asked if she had seen Jonesy. Bernice hadn't seen him yet today, but she knew that "Unc" was supposed to have Colombian grass brought into Blackston by some Puerto Rican connections. She delivered the verdict that it was OK stuff, burned a little, made you very high very quickly, but didn't last long. All in all it was better than the stuff that some of the soldiers had brought back from Vietnam. The "Vietnam Red," as it was called, burned your throat raw. The best Bernice had had recently was brought up by Uncle Jonesy's niece from South Carolina. No matter where it came from, Darla knew she could sell it.

Darla was careful and discreet in selling the stuff, but she knew the cops didn't really care about grass sales or use, so she didn't worry about being arrested. She kept it hidden in the apartment, and after it had been dried, crushed, sorted, and packaged into small brown $5 packets, she carried it around with her. You never knew when you might make a sale, on the street, on the way to the grocery store or the liquor store, or near the pool hall on the corner. You could even sit on the front steps and smoke in this area, though many of the people who used it wouldn't think of doing that. Lots of people, mostly older people like Aunt Bea or even her own mother, didn't like other people to know that they smoked grass, so they did so only in their own homes. Yet the young people like Bea's niece or Dulcie felt they couldn't smoke at home because of their parents' attitudes. Selling grass was a good way of knowing who was doing what behind the façade of law-abiding respectability on this subject.

Randy would probably be bothering her to get some money. He didn't really like grass and hardly ever smoked it. She'd have to be careful that Randy didn't try to sneak some away and sell it on his own. Since heroin was harder to get, Randy needed more money more often so he could be in the right place with money in hand to buy, or "cop," when it became available. Things were getting so tight that Randy and Jim B. were even talking about signing up for methadone. Big Jack was holding out. Darla hoped he could talk some sense into Randy. Everyone she knew who was on methadone seemed too messed up and crazy-acting, including that Jimmy from down the block, who must have made twenty trips past her house on his way to and from the pool hall in the last hour, talking all that shit so loud and unable to slow down.

Jimmy was lucky. He didn't hustle at all, or at least not much. His mother and wife took care of him. Jimmy must be near forty, maybe more, and he'd been using heroin since before Darla had moved here. Jimmy's mother owned that tenement she lived in, and her family lived in five of the apartments—Jimmy and his wife in the first-floor front, his mother in the rear, two of Jimmy's cousins and their husbands and children on the second floor, and his aunt on the third floor. Darla sure didn't know where Jimmy's mother ever got the money to buy a house, but she had, and she took care of it.

Jimmy's wife wasn't around much. She went off to work every day, and the only time you really saw her was on the weekend. She always got drunk on Saturday night, and she and Jimmy would fight. That woman sure could holler and scream. All day Saturday she would be up and down the street to the store, talking to people, playing with the kids and buying candy for them. But come Saturday night she'd be drunk. Then back to work on Monday morning.

Darla couldn't understand how anyone kept working week after week. Maybe it was because Jimmy's wife had no children of her own to look after. She was always playing with kids in the neighborhood, buying them sodas and ice cream. Darla couldn't imagine what it would be like not to have kids. She loved all of hers. The new baby looked just like Randy. He was already handsome and only a few weeks old. Carolee was becoming a young lady, a four-year-old charmer. And she loved Bobby with his bedwetting and his shy ways equally well. Without children Darla wouldn't feel alive. Ever since her first child was born when she was sixteen, the children, the home she made for them, her status as a mother were the most important things in her life. The children provided the focus around which her life was organized, and caring for them was her single pressing responsibility.

Darla and Belvie were unable to find Jonesy, so they didn't work out anything about the grass, but they knew Jonesy would come get them as soon as he had some, and he always knew where to find them. In fact, he sometimes spent hours watching TV with them or playing checkers. He'd been less able to do this lately since he'd taken to selling hamburgers, fish sandwiches, and french fries out of the kitchen in Hank's basement.

Darla could keep one eye on the basement from her first floor window just across the street and like many people in Blackston, particularly women, she spent a lot of time watching the events of the street from her window. She hoped Jonesy would turn up soon with something to sell since she really needed some money before check day. On that day, either the first or fifteenth of the month, Aid to Dependent Children payments from the social-services department were delivered in Blackston by mailmen traveling in pairs. The mailmen feared attack by thieves or by some desperately irate person whose check did not arrive for whatever reasons. Check day brought many changes to Blackston. Many women and not a few men stood in doorways and on stoops waiting for the mailman's arrival. Long lines formed outside of privately owned check-cashing services that charged a percentage of each check for cashing them. Not many Blackstonians had accounts at commercial banks, so most had to use the check-cashing services. Prices went up in local supermarkets on this day, but despite this well-known and often documentated state of affairs, the stores were crowded with shoppers.

Check day was still two days off. Darla hadn't seen Randy much today, but she was sure he didn't have any money to help her out. He had left the house very early, even before she and the kids were up. When Randy was hustling and on drugs, he spent most of his time on the streets, and he often ate only once a day. Darla cooked as large an amount of food as possible for an indeterminate number of people so there was always something for Randy if he wanted it and for friends if he brought some home. If he didn't eat, other people might stop by, and they would be offered food or it would be put away for the next day. In fact, lunch today would probably be warmed-up greens and neck bones from last night. The baby could drink the juice from the pot, and Carolee had been eating greens and chewing on neck bones since she was about a year old.

Randy's not being around the house much made it a lot easier to deal with the welfare social worker and other people who came around asking about who all was in the family. Darla was especially concerned, since not so long ago she had told the welfare that the baby's father was someone she had met casually at a dance and not seen since. Those welfare people couldn't possibly believe such stories, but they wrote it down and couldn't do much else about it. Fortunately, Darla had registered with the welfare under her married name and received her checks under that name. This meant that when she went into the hospital and used her health card for identification, the name entered in the legal records, including that on the child's birth-certificate application from the hospital, was Burton, Darla's legal married name. A lot of women Darla knew used their identification with maiden name to apply for welfare. When their babies were born, they were given the mother's maiden name on the hospital records, the welfare rolls, and the birth certificate. But for $15 you could have a name change made later with the city birth-record bureau so that the child would have his father's name, and the welfare department need never know.

The latest people who had been around from the outside asking questions were that White man and his Black partner who said they were from the Census Bureau. The Black man had done all the talking, but Darla could tell who was boss. She laughed to think that they had really expected her to tell them whether there was a man living in the house. Maybe they weren't related to the welfare or any other agency, as they said, but once you gave them information and they wrote it down, you didn't know where it went or who used it. It was safer not to tell, so Darla said she was the head of the household. On official papers Blackston must look as if it had nothing except women at the head of the household. Why, even while Randy was getting a welfare payment as an addict certified as unemployable, he had it sent to another address. Besides, having a different address allowed him to claim housing costs. This came to about $60 a month after he had paid the man whose address he was using $10 or $15 each time a check arrived. The welfare checks had stopped when the social-services department insisted that Randy sign up for a drug therapy program. In addition, the man whose address Randy used wanted more than $10 each time he took the check from the mailman and held it for Randy. Randy, on the other hand, would rather do without the check than be ripped off by this person whose only value to Randy was that he had an address and a mailbox to claim as his own.

Darla had talked with Uncle Jonesy about the Census Bureau people, and she knew that he objected to the whole idea that anyone deserved or was entitled to information about him. Jonesy just outright refused to talk to anyone asking questions. He had been one of the first to throw away the yellow forms received in the mail from the Census Bureau. But most others followed quickly, and yellow scraps were evident in the garbage cans up and down the street for days. Maybe that was why these two men had come trying to get the information by knocking on doors and asking.

Jonesy was not the only one who objected to having strangers know anything about him. Darla had already taught Bobby not to answer, to shrug his shoulders or say "I don't know" when anyone came asking for any family member. Carolee had better learn soon to be quiet too. Darla had seen groups of children and adults stand silent and unhelpful when the person inquired about was right there or known to be close by. Even small children learned to recognize and deceive the bill collectors, insurance men, landlords, and undercover or plainclothes police who came asking questions.

Yet within the community of neighbors, friends, and kin, most people knew or could know with a minimum of effort more about each other than was imagined by outsiders. Sitting in the windows or on stoops, watching the comings and goings of hundreds of people just on this block, talking about events and neighborhood crises, searching up local examples to illustrate discussions of "right" and "wrong" behavior, family arguments that moved out onto porch or stoop and could be heard through open windows on hot days, kin ties that spanned many households—all contributed to a situation where people who were seen by outsiders as "not knowing their next-door neighbors" were in reality very aware of and knowledgeable about a wide range of interpersonal relationships and events.

AS DARLA PILED a box full of the children's clothes into Hank's panel truck, it was hard to believe that a whole year had passed since the fire across the street that had wrecked Hank and Bernice's house. Darla could look across the street and see that the first-floor windows that had been covered with boards for months were now shielded only by drapes. Everyone on Paul Street covered their windows in some way. Darla herself looked back at her own torn green window shade on the one window and the blanket that was nailed up over the other. She'd better go get that blanket now while Belvie and Jim B. helped to move her few pieces of furniture into the back of the truck. Hank had offered to help her move, but he had gone off to do something else while they loaded the truck. Since the job was almost finished, Darla sat down on the stoop and looked around.

Darla didn't like to remember this past year. It had been so full of so many changes, and most ot them had been bad. That was one of the reasons she had decided to move away from Paul Street. And the welfare hadn't objected when she found a third-floor walkup apartment several miles to the north of here. Darla felt her troubles had begun last spring when Randy had decided to give up heroin and start on methadone. He wasn't actually giving it up. There just wasn't much heroin on the street. And the hospital-sponsored methadone clinic gave the stuff away for free. Randy's friend Jim B. had joined him in registering for the methadone program.

As Darla saw things, it was after Randy had begun using methadone that his actions really became crazy. Unlike heroin, the stuff seemed to make him act wild—full of energy, tense, and not even feeling good. Randy had told her that to get back a good feeling he needed to drink too. This was the same Randy who had laughed at people who drank when he was on heroin. Then he used to drink a little wine occasionally. But now he began to drink wine, hard liquor, or anything he could get every day. It hadn't been pleasant to have him around the house any more. Besides, his nerves seemed so jumpy that he didn't want to stay still for long either, so he was always out and around, sometimes going up and down the street with Jimmy or Jim B. Even his friend Jack, who had refused to go near methadone, didn't want to have much to do with Randy any more.

Randy had begun spending more and more time with those people doing the study. When she complained to him about this, Randy always told her that he was just helping them with their work. And he was doing it because they could help him. He had even showed her a fancy letter they had written to the Legal Aid lawyers saying that Randy was now in a methadone maintenance program and helping them with their project and that they had hope that he would be a useful community member. Maybe that kind of thing could help. After all, Randy had two charges pending. But Darla didn't want him to spend so much time around that woman.

Darla remembered that she had run into Miz Valentine down at Wilma's house and had complained about the change in Randy then. Darla also remembered saying at that time that she wished Randy were back on heroin because he was a nicer person with heroin than with methadone and alcohol. Both Wilma and Miz Valentine had seemed shocked at this statement. But Darla had insisted that it was true.

Anyway things had gone from bad to worse. Randy seemed very moody. He would have fights with anyone, including his own brother. Before this Randy had always been so lighthearted and fun to be with. Darla was sure that everyone on Paul Street knew that Randy was an addict, yet he had had lots of friends. People still seemed to like him, even though they too would talk about the change in him. As far as Darla could see, the change had come about when he started taking methadone.

Darla had been terrified when Randy was shot in the leg by a drug dealer. Randy told her that he had been trying to chase the man out of the neighborhood. She couldn't understand what was going on with Randy. Even before his leg was healed, he had broken into the apartment of the anthropologists and stolen several things. She knew because Randy brought the stereo set to her. In fact, it was about the only item worth much among the things she was moving today.

Darla had spent most of her married life here on Paul Street, and she had three lovely children all born here. But she now had many sad and angry memories too. It was here that Randy had begun to get into more and more trouble. He had had the fight with the drug dealer. It was while he was still hobbling around with a crutch after the shooting that he had used the crutch to break the window of that woman's car. Jim B. had described to her the fight that followed when the man in the car beat up on Randy. It seemed to be some kind of lovers' quarrel, and Darla was embarrassed that Randy was being so violent and so public about all these things. Then he had slashed the tires on a car belonging to a man who lived in the rehabilitated city-owned building across the street. Darla never even knew what the fight was all about, but she had heard that the man planned to deal with Randy with a tire iron when he caught him. The man never got a chance to do so because Randy's actions finally landed him in jail on a forty-five-day sentence for harassment.

Darla didn't even go to visit him during that time. There was no public transportation that went anywhere near the detention center. She had gone to see him just before they sent him away to serve his sentence. He told her at that time that he had declared himself an addict on his arrest sheet and therefore would continue to receive methadone in jail. Darla hadn't liked this at all, but there was nothing she could do about it.

For Darla it had been a real shock but still a pleasure to see Randy again even before his time was up. He seemed more like his old self. They had shaved off his large, beautiful Afro, and he looked like he had when they got married or after he was drafted and they had cut his hair. He had gained some weight on jail food too. And at least for the first few days he seemed like his old re- laxed, loving, joking self. He explained to her that while in jail he had been in several fights and they had transferred him to the jail hospital for tests. The psychiatrist and social workers had then sent him to the county hospital, where they kept him on heavy doses of tranquilizers. Randy, who had always been resourceful, escaped easily.

It was Randy's father who had come to tell them that the

hospital authorities had called his house to report Randy's escape and to ask Mr. Burton to cooperate in getting Randy back to the hospital. Beyond delivering the message, Mr. Burton told them—and said he had also told the hospital—that his son was twenty-four years old and would have to make his own decisions.

Randy was picked up by the police and returned to the hospital a few days later. When his father and sister visited him there, they reported to Darla that he was so doped up that he looked and acted like a zombie. Mr. Burton had been totally unsuccessful in his attempt to get the ward authorities to tell him what kind of treatment, if any, Randy was receiving or why he had to be doped so heavily. It was now past the deadline of his jail term, and Mr. Burton didn't understand the basis on which Randy was being kept in the hospital.

No one in Randy's family was either surprised or willing to turn him back when Randy escaped for a second time and returned to his home on Paul Street with Darla. With a little help from his friends, Randy had gone back to using both methadone and alcohol. But Darla was so glad to have him back that even this didn't bother her at first. It was just a week after his second escape from the hospital when Randy was shot.

Darla sat on the stoop just a door away from where it all happened and remembered as best she could. She hadn't been in the house or even on the block when the shooting took place. She had taken the children over to her mother's house in a different section of the city and had planned to leave them there for the weekend. She had wanted to spend some time alone with Randy now that he was back. Jim B. and Belvie had called her mother's house from the police station to tell her that Randy had been shot and was in serious condition at the Jewish hospital near Blackston. They offered to meet her at the hospital and tell her what they knew. Darla had agreed, and her mother had paid for a service car to take her to the hospital.

At the hospital Darla had had to talk with a detective and a policeman who were there, but she didn't even now remember most of what they had asked. It wasn't until after they had talked to her that she had been allowed to see Randy. The entire top of his head was covered with a white bandage and his eyes were closed. He looked dead already. Only his chest moved a little. But it looked as if one of the many machines attached to him was pumping even that small amount of movement into him. Darla had talked to him, but Randy didn't seem to hear her. And then a doctor had taken Darla out to the main door of the intensive care unit and begun to talk about his small chance for life, the need for total care if he lived, loss of eyesight, and other phrases that Darla had tried to remember when she talked with her mother later. But right now she didn't really want to hear any of them.

Although it was past midnight Darla, Belvie, and Jim B. had decided to walk the dozen blocks back to their homes on Paul Street so that they could talk about what had happened. Jim B. and Belvie explained that they had been with Randy at Dulcie's apartment on the third floor in their building. A card game had been going on. People were eating and drinking and playing cards around the kitchen table. Neither Belvie nor Jim B. had been in the card game. They were sitting in the front room talking with some friends. Neither of them knew exactly what had happened, but they had heard a fight start between Randy and an old friend of his sisters' named Joey King. Randy had been noisy and abusive, and Joey King was drinking and unpleasant. Randy had left the apartment threatening to return with a knife. But he had only come back as far as the front door of the apartment when Joey King had taken a small gun out of the purse that his woman friend had on the table in front of her. He fired a single shot across the kitchen and hit Randy in the head. Then Joey King had bolted from the room, jumped across Randy's body, and run down three flights of stairs to the street. Belvie ran to the rear apartment on the second floor, where the only phone in the building was, and called for an ambulance and for the police. Several other people left before either an ambulance or a police car arrived. Belvie and Jim B. had stayed beside Randy, but they hadn't known what to do for him. Jim B. said it was a horrible sight. When all three of them reached Paul Street, the warm-weather, Friday-night life of visiting, gossiping, drinking, and partying was not totally over. Many people stopped them to ask about Randy.

Darla remembered that she had made a number of trips to the hospital during the three days after the shooting. That woman, Miz Valentine, had gone with her a few times. Darla didn't especially like that woman, but she had felt and even expressed her feeling that the both of them really cared about Randy. Darla had talked about how much fun it had been to be with Randy—he was warm, outgoing, friendly, amusing, saying and doing things to make her laugh. Both Belvie and Miz Valentine had listened and understood while Darla repeated some of the things Randy had said and done within the past week. Although they mentioned it, nobody had really wanted to think of Randy as blind and helpless. Belvie had changed the talk around. Darla even remembered that they had put a record on the stolen stereo set to keep the apartment from seeming so dead. Even Randy's theft didn't seem to matter to either of them now.

Then on Tuesday—Darla would always remember that day—Randy had died.

For almost fifty years Thaddeus Burton had been a quiet man. Now, sitting here beside the body of his youngest son, he remained quiet. But inside of him a voice raged and wanted to cry out, to scream, to ask what had gone wrong and to know, "Would things have been different had Eva lived and been with me to raise these children?"

Thaddeus Burton had always been a handsome man. His straight, somewhat sharp facial features seemed to contrast with his coal-black skin and his gray hair, which he kept only moderately long even in this time of blooming Afros. His own family background, combined with many years as a servant, had produced a dignified, almost reserved outer manner. Yet it was more than an outer manner that had enabled him to spend the past few days talking with Randy's wife, his own kin, the anthropologist, and friends while Randy lay near death in the hospital. He had sincerely tried to comfort others and to reassure them that they as individuals could not have changed the course of events that had led to this tragedy. An inner gentleness, a caring for others, and optimism had kept him going through many hard years and stayed with him now. Unfortunately, he wasn't as comforting or reassuring to himself as he thought back over the past quarter century of his own life.

Thaddeus had been forty when Randy and his twin brother

Stanford were born. Thaddeus's wife, Eva, was only twenty-four at that time. Yet just four years later cancer had taken her away. He had been left with a family of four. Johneva, their first-born, had come unexpectedly, even before they were married. Thaddeus Jr. had been born while his father was still in the army and stationed overseas. Eva's mother wasn't happy about the match or her illegitimate granddaughter. She had always prided herself on her family's being respectable. Thaddeus never thought of Eva as anything but the most respectable of women. He knew that she had never been intimate with another man, and he insisted that they get married as soon as he came back. They hadn't parted from then on. When Johneva, who was named after her mother, was about two they had a son and named him Thaddeus Jr. Then, four happy years later, Randolph and Stanford were born. From the day of their birth, Thaddeus had wondered how two identical twins could be so alike and yet so different.

Life had been so good for them all then. He still had lots of snapshots taken during this time: pictures of Eva and her daughter, who looked so much alike; of Eva and Thaddeus Jr., who looked exactly like his father; pictures of himself and Eva alone, with the twins, at parties, in the park near the housing project where they lived.

He and Eva had been so happy then. He had always had a job and had no trouble finding another during this period. Occasionally he tried to supplement their income with poker winnings, and more often than not he won, because he was both skillful and lucky. But Eva preferred that the two of them spend his spare time together or that he stay home with his family even though it might mean a little less money to spend on the children or the house. She herself stayed at home and took care of the family rather than work at the few low-paying kinds of jobs available to a Black woman.

Then death had come and taken Eva away from him just as it had now taken Randy twenty-four years later. He thought back on those twenty-four years. Never during that time had he seriously considered marrying again. Immediately after his wife's funeral, he knew that he wanted to keep his family together and with him, to raise them up in a single household. But he wasn't able to do this at first all by himself. He had to keep working to provide for them, so the children went to live with their mother's mother in a very respectable middle-income section of the city.

Thaddeus realized that he could no longer go from job to job. He had to work at two jobs, pay all the children's expenses, and see them only on weekends. Sometimes he thought that his mother-in-law gave the children more discipline than love, but he had to admit they were growing up into clean, mannerly, healthy children.

When Johneva was almost twelve, he was able to take the children to live with him. They moved to Blackston and became one of the first Black families on a block that was still predominantly working-class and Jewish. Johneva helped take care of the small four-room apartment and the younger children. Thaddeus continued to work as house servant, chauffeur, and general helper for at least two well-to-do White families in the city. Although the wages weren't especially good, the work wasn't too demanding. Occasionally he could take the children to work with him, and there was always a good supply of cast-off clothing for his family.

During this period card playing provided his only entertainment and adult social life, as well as a supplement to his income.

Thaddeus tried to be both mother and father to the children. He really loved them even though he wasn't always able to show it. He was always quiet and gentle, and he believed in talking to children rather than beating on them. The only one of his children who had always been a problem was Randy. He was noisy, always ready to argue, always getting into trouble, while his twin brother, Stanford, was quiet and less outgoing. They were all beautiful children, but the novelty of the twins appealed to Thaddeus's employers and their friends, who often bought gifts for the twins and invited them to spend a day in some expensive townhouse or to visit for a week in the country. Randy remained the more adventuresome on these occasions too, and so in the pictures Thaddeus kept in a scrapbook, it was Randy, not Stanford, who was riding the horse during their summer visit to the farm home of a well-to-do artist. Another picture from this visit showed the twins scrubbed and fancy in new matching pajamas sitting in bed on either side of their host's young daughter. Thaddeus was always amused when years later Randy would point to

this picture and wink broadly as he told people how he had been
to bed with a White girl before he was ten.

Randy had always been especially dear to Thaddeus. He really
didn't mind making all those trips to the school that Randy's
behavior seemed to require, but he had never felt he could do
much. The principal and the teachers all said they thought Randy
was very bright, but they couldn't discipline him. Occasionally
some administrator would talk around the fact that there was no
mother in the home, that Randy came from a male-headed family, as though this was peculiar in a Black community. But this
never made much sense to Thaddeus, since Stanford, Thaddeus
Jr., and Johneva were all doing well in school.

Then, after being a substitute mother so long, Johneva became
a real mother at the age of sixteen. She dropped out of school.
There were no programs then as there were now that allowed
young pregnant girls to remain in school. If there had been, Jonnie would probably have remained, since she had always liked
school and done well in her courses. But with a tiny baby to care
for, she had less time to keep after Randy, and Thaddeus wasn't
surprised when a short time later Randy began to stay away from
school more and more and finally stopped going altogether.

So much seemed to be happening at once, more than Thaddeus
felt he could deal with. He had to keep his jobs in order to provide
for the family, even though this often meant he was gone in the
evenings when his employers were giving dinners or parties and
sometimes on Saturday or Sunday too when an employer
telephoned to ask for some special favor or help. His employers
provided the phone in his home so they could reach Thaddeus at
any time. They even called and lent his services to their friends.
The tips he received never made up for the time he had to spend
away from his family.

Sitting here beside Randy's coffin, Thaddeus wished he had
thought then to do what he did more often now: have someone
else answer the phone and say, "Thaddeus isn't home." He
remembered Randy's feelings about it all, since Randy had never
been hesitant about expressing them loudly. Randy had felt that
his father was exploited. He often said he would never do the
things his father had to do to earn a living. And he was even a lit-

tle ashamed of Thaddeus's way of getting out of overtime work by pretending not to be at home. If it were up to Randy he would have told all of them off, especially the widow who wanted more and more of Thaddeus's time since her husband died.

Thaddeus could understand a little how Randy felt. But Randy never seemed to understand the world as Thaddeus saw it. After all, Thaddeus had had no particular skill when he started working almost twenty years ago for this same employer. Randy, the grade-school dropout, was especially proud that his father had gone to Morgan State Teachers Preparatory School for one year. The army had ended that. Then he had begun a family. Eva had died, and Thaddeus needed steady work that he could count on to provide for his children. So there he was, an intelligent, quiet, respectable Black man with no particular skill and a desperate need for steady work. He took the only work he could find and had been working for one of his employers for twenty years. He had done his best. Yet in his heart and head he felt that his best had not been enough. But he didn't know what more he could have done. Here was his youngest son in a coffin at the age of twenty-four, even younger than his mother had been when she died.

With a combination of hard, steady work, extra jobs, and winnings from his card playing, Thaddeus felt he had done a reasonable job of providing for his family. He had never applied for or received welfare in his life. After Johneva had her baby, she applied for and received small welfare payments for herself and the baby. Thaddeus tried not to think about all the things that had happened to Johneva after she had moved out of the family home—marriage, desertion, drug addiction, hospitalization, and two more children. But through it all Johneva had kept up a strong interest in Randy and her other brothers. She never moved far away. She had tried many times over to talk to Thaddeus Jr. and Randy, to persuade them that drugs were not a solution. And although she had been able to cure herself, she wasn't able to persuade Thaddeus Jr. or Randy that they should never start on drugs—to do as she said, not as she did. Thank goodness Jonnie was back at home raising her three sons and caring for the third-floor walkup she and they shared with her father. In part, it was the welfare money Jonnie received that enabled Thaddeus to work less and to be "out" more often when his employers called with overtime demands.

THADDEUS JR.'S REACTION to Randy's death had been anger—anger at the whole damn world, including this lousy slum he and Randy had spent their whole lives in and couldn't seem to get out of, except to go to prison; anger at the young fools who carried around and played with knives and guns; anger at that particular bastard, his own sister's ex-boyfriend, who had shot Randy in the head even though he had known for years that Randy acted wild and had never seriously hurt anyone; anger at the mental hospital that only drugged Randy but hadn't worked to help him or even keep him from running away again; anger at his own father for being so calm and reasonable—and finally anger at himself for caring so much and crying so much.

All his life Thaddeus Jr. had worked hard to control himself. Although he was only two years older than Randy, he had acted like a big brother for many years and had tried to get Randy to be more like himself. Both he and Randy had been heroin addicts. Yet up to the day he died Randy would have shot some heroin if it was offered, while Thaddeus knew that he would never shoot the stuff again. But Thaddeus also knew he had no scruples about selling heroin to others if he thought he could make some money quickly and be fairly safe from arrest. Unlike Randy, Thaddeus had a single-minded goal: to get money to get away from Paul Street and out of Blackston.

Both he and Randy had been in jail, though at different times in different places, and up to the day he died Randy stood a good chance of going back to jail, while Thaddeus knew that he would never go back if it were at all under his control. Both he and Randy had learned to gamble together, to cheat at craps, to hustle pool, to play poker, to take part in the games of chance offered by traveling hustlers who carried their boards and cards and dice from street to street in Blackston. Yet Randy had always been more impulsive, skillful but less concentrated, more willing to go on to something else, especially if he was losing. Thaddeus was perhaps more skillful and exercised great control over all of his actions, except the ability to stop gambling, whether he was winning or losing.

Thaddeus often joined his father's card games. The two of them related as equals; both were reserved and calm. Randy's relations with his father had always been more sporadic but emotional and very junior-senior in manner.

Thaddeus Jr. didn't believe that you could or should try to control anyone's actions other than your own. The only exceptions he had made to this were his recent unsuccessful attempts in relation to Randy. His attempts during this past year to interact with others to tone down Randy's increasingly wild behavior had been unsuccessful. Thaddeus had exercised great self-control in talking to and spending time with Darla and that anthropologist, neither of whom he liked very much, to discuss Randy's behavior and to get and make suggestions about what might be done to get Randy off methadone and into some kind of treatment. He had to exercise even greater self-control to interact with Randy. One night he and Randy had been playing craps together as they used to but Randy had been called for cheating his own brother. Randy's reaction—to start a fist fight with Thaddeus and to run away—hadn't been at all reasonable. Thaddeus didn't think he would ever become involved in someone else's life like that again. It went against his whole way of relating to the world and had ended in Randy's death. Thaddeus's own love for his brother and his great desire to be helpful hadn't changed anything.

From now on, Thaddeus told his wife, he wasn't going to become involved with anyone. He was only going to control himself, to keep working at that deadly job at the plant, to get where he could there, and to make enough money in any other way he could think of so that he could get his family off of Paul Street.

Other Hard Work: The Wards

OSCAR JUST DIDN'T understand these women. Here was his sister-in-law Bea throwing him out of her house again. Other people in the neighborhood might call her Aunt Bea, but he didn't even want to be related to her at times like this. He felt he hadn't done anything—at least nothing much—just cursed a little. Anyway,

Bea cursed more than he did. She sure could be mean when she was drinking. And Oscar, Bea, and Mr. Jay had been drinking since this morning. Bea must have had some money. She had sent Mr. Jay over to the liquor store, and Oscar had decided to join the party when he saw Mr. Jay walking back with a bottle held up under his coat.

One reason Oscar felt specially bad about being thrown out was that he had no other place to go. It was still too cold to be sitting out on that stone stoop. And he knew his wife, Gloria, didn't want to have him upstairs. She had said so just before he came down to Bea's.

Gloria would rather be surrounded by all those daughters and their friends and grandchildren. They all listened more to her than they listened to Oscar. In fact, his two sons weren't living in the house now partly because they didn't get along with him too well either. His older son, Raymond, preferred to rent one of Bea's three rooms, where he had privacy and didn't have to argue all the time, as he told his mother. And Edward, the younger one, who even contributed something to his mother each week since he started working at the same place as his father, claimed to live at home but spent more time staying with friends. Right now Oscar didn't give a damn where any of them slept. Nobody showed him any respect.

Hell, he was their father. So he was a bit of a drinker. In fact he drank a lot. Still, he had managed to keep the same job for twenty-four years. During all that time he had provided for six children, relatives that Gloria had taken in from time to time, and now grandchildren. Oscar had mixed feelings about his work. It was his life in many ways. Twenty-four years with the same company had meant factory work, loading-platform work, and finally his present job as a delivery-truck driver. But he also knew that after twenty-four years at the same job he made only three-fourths as much money as any garbage man in this city who had just begun working this year. Oscar knew that he wasn't the right color to get a job as a garbage man. They hadn't had any Black people in that job when he started work in this city, and they had few even now. He had read about their salaries in the paper last year when the garbage men were going on strike. And he knew it partly because Gloria kept reminding him about it. He sure felt tired.

He wasn't going to let them push him around. He'd go upstairs anyways and go to sleep on that bed that filled most of his and Gloria's room. They couldn't keep him out of there. Often he wished he could get Gloria to do something else with him there too. But instead she built up a living wall of babies between them whenever they were both in the same bed. He hadn't been able to make love to his wife in longer than he could remember.

Oscar stumbled up the steps and gripped the wobbly handrail. At the second floor he pushed against his apartment door, brushed past the people crowded into the communal kitchen of the apartment, and went into the back bedroom. He climbed into bed with all his clothes on. And now he couldn't sleep. It wasn't the noise that bothered him. He was used to living with six or seven adults and a shifting number of children in the four-room apartment. He couldn't sleep because he wasn't drunk enough. Damn it, he wanted a bottle of his own. But he knew he'd never get Gloria to give him money for liquor. During all these years he would try to keep back $10 or $20 before giving Gloria his paycheck. Sometimes he wasn't able to do so before Gloria took the money for the house, or he spent it before the weekend ended or lent money to his friends and like today was without a drink when he wanted one.

Too bad he hadn't had more to drink before Bea threw him out of her three rooms on the floor below. He would have taken more but Bea was sneaky. She kept the bottle closed and down on the floor by her chair. She was always trying to keep him from drinking, even when she was drinking a lot more than he got. Damn if he was going to beg her for a drink.

He couldn't go to sleep. Instead his mind seemed to wander back to those early days when he was just up from the South and had met Gloria. She was so pretty then—small and light-skinned with long "good" (unkinky) hair and a sweet smile. Everyone who looked at that picture of the two of them on the rooftop shortly before they got married agreed she was pretty. He enjoyed carrying the picture around in his wallet and showing it to everyone. Right now Oscar felt Gloria would be prettier if she would just have her missing front teeth replaced. But he knew better than to try to get his wife to do anything she didn't want to do.

That stubbornness ran in her family. You could see it in Bea.

And it sure was passed on to their oldest daughter, Brenda. She was dark like him, pretty like her mother, quiet, and stubborn as a mule. She had been stubborn when she got pregnant after high school and decided not to marry the baby's father. He had wanted to marry Brenda. He had come around often and brought things for the baby. Brenda had called him when she needed anything, but she had stubbornly refused to marry him. What she had done instead was to get welfare support for the baby, move into a place of her own, and go to work in an insurance company office. Gloria took care of the baby during the day until Brenda returned from work. Then Brenda would take her little girl, Roberta, back to her own apartment about eight blocks away.

Brenda was stubborn about other things too. She wouldn't do any art work even though she was good at it. The things she had done in high school had won some prizes. Gloria's wealthy employer had asked to "borrow" some pieces such as the sculptured head to display in his apartment. But Brenda just didn't seem to care about art work now. Sometimes that streak of stubbornness helped. Brenda put money in the bank every pay-day and absolutely refused to let it be used except for what she had in mind. The stubbornness was in Roberta too. It was hard to believe that his first grandchild, who liked to be called Bobby, was now in school herself. Her mother had finally married the son of good friends. Now she, her husband, Bobby, and the new twins lived in this same building. Oscar supposed that the money Brenda had put in the bank had gone into furniture after the wedding. But he didn't know for sure. Nobody ever told him anything.

At one time Oscar had hoped that a son might be closer to him. He was pleased when their second child turned out to be a boy. He was a good-looking and healthy baby. Gloria had insisted on naming him Raymond after her own father. Somehow Oscar and his first son had never become very close. Then Ann was born. It wasn't until after they had a second son that Oscar got to name a boy after himself, Oscar Edward Ward. Still, Edward looked and acted more like his mother. After Edward II came Gertrude Gloria, named for her mother but better known as Gert. Finally, their "change" baby, Naomi, had been born when Gloria was forty.

Maybe the reason Oscar hadn't ever become very close to any of his children was that Gloria provided all the love and attention they seemed to need. And most of the time Oscar was at work or out drinking with his friends. Oscar felt good that he had kept his job throughout this time of babies and moves from one place to another. He had stayed at the same job even though the company he worked for had changed owners three times. Each time the union had also changed, and each time Oscar lost his union seniority and benefits. But he had supported his growing family as best he could. Only occasionally, between children and after the first-born daughter, Brenda, was big enough to help look after the younger ones, did Gloria do some domestic work in the White suburbs.

Oscar finally felt himself dropping off to sleep, still thinking about his family.

Meanwhile, out in the kitchen, most of the female members of Oscar's family were doing their own things. Naomi, a pre-teenager, the youngest but by no means the smallest of the Ward sisters, was still at that age where all the other males and females, family and friends, were constantly telling her to do something. Naomi, find my blue shoes! Answer the door! Give me my cigarettes, there they are on the sink! Feed the dogs! Bring me a Pamper! So although it was fine in some ways to be a part of the give and take of grownup interaction, Naomi clearly took more than she was allowed to give.

One of the people who bothered Naomi the most with her bossy, pushy orders was Little Ann, mother of her brother Edward's baby. Little Ann had moved into the Wards' four-room apartment when she became pregnant while she was still in her late teens. Edward, who had quit school without graduating, after several unsuccessful attempts to find an acceptable trade at a technical school of his choice, had met Little Ann through friends. After quitting school Edward volunteered for service in the navy. He came out of the navy with no more of a lead to a job than when he left the trade school. But in the meantime he did begin a family and brought Little Ann back to his parents' home.

Little Ann was called that to distinguish her from Ann, the second-oldest girl in the Ward family. Naomi didn't need any help in telling the two apart. Her own sister Ann used Naomi too, but for the most part Ann was quiet, even-tempered, and less bossy. Ann was really very different from Little Ann. Naomi felt that Little Ann pushed her around as if she owned her. And now that Little Ann was pregnant again she was more trouble than ever. Even the whine in her voice seemed uglier. Naomi was angry because Little Ann lived there, ate there, and didn't do any work.

Naomi wasn't alone in her view of Little Ann. All the other girls were bothered by her surly, bossy ways. Edward, who had brought this all about, didn't spend much time at home. He sometimes slept there only a few nights a week. So he missed most of Little Ann's troublemaking. And most of the time Little Ann was smart enough not to bother Mrs. Ward with her troubles.

Gert, Naomi's next older sister, wasn't bossed around by Little Ann. Gert was also pregnant and not inclined to give one inch to Little Ann's demands. Gert and Little Ann shared the second bedroom with Ann, Naomi, and their friend Clara, who had moved out of her parents' home across the street after a family fight. Some of this sharing was made possible by informal sleeping shifts. Ann, who was a clerical trainee in a downtown investment company, left the house early in the morning, as did Naomi, who was still in elementary school. Little Ann and Gert and Clara often slept through the morning, sometimes into the early afternoon, and consequently went to bed much later than Naomi or Ann.

Gert was officially still in school although she didn't often get there. She went to a special program operated by the public school system for girls who became pregnant while still students. The emphasis of the program was on preparing for the coming baby through courses on hygiene, nutrition, and child care. Conventional school work in academic subjects was secondary. Gert was only slightly more interested in the child-care lessons than she had been in her regular school work. She knew the baby would come whether she went to school and learned about it or not. She knew the baby would be fed and raised in this household where any number of babies had been fed and raised before. Whether she went to nutrition and child-care classes didn't seem very important.

Gert knew these things the same way she had known she would

get pregnant someday. She remembered talking to Naomi's god-mother about this over a year ago. Bettylou had asked her then whether she used or planned to use anything for birth control. Gert's answer then had been "no" to both questions, and they joked about how soon it would be till Gert became pregnant. Gert knew that whenever it happened she wouldn't be unhappy about it. But she sure as hell was a little tired of it now. Her breasts were hurting, and she knew she'd be even bigger and more uncomfortable when the weather got hot.

Gert was the most outspoken of the Ward girls. She remembered that when she was about eleven years old and Bettylou and Val were moving onto the block, she had been one of the first people to talk to them. If she hadn't introduced them to her mother, Naomi might not have them as godparents now. Then she had called them Miz Val and Mr. Val. Now she only called them that to tease them. Gert enjoyed teasing people, insulting them, or otherwise being outspoken, even provocative in speech. Sometimes this got her into trouble, particularly at school. But shit, she couldn't help it if people couldn't take it.

Putting her thoughts into action, Gert started in on Naomi, who pouted and called to her mother to say that Gert was bothering her again. Ann's reaction to the fuss was to get up from the table and go into the living room to watch the TV set that played nonstop throughout the day. Gloria turned from the stove where she was cooking and gave a half-hearted order to Gert to stop bothering her sister. She then turned to Naomi and told her to stop making a fuss. Gloria could and did raise her voice and demand attention and action when she felt it was needed. But she reacted to this momentary hassling with only momentary attention and conviction. Then she went back to her conversation with Dee Dee, her next-door neighbor, who often spent hours here in the Wards' kitchen.

Dee Dee and Gloria continued to talk about their experiences with the nearby hospital. It was a Jewish hospital which now had many Black and Spanish patients, especially in the older section of wards and in the clinics. Gloria had had a great deal of experience in dealing with health institutions and seemed to get a certain delight in discussing illnesses, injuries, diagnoses, and treatments.

Dee Dee, somewhat older than Gloria's grown daughters but younger than Gloria, was often able to relate and interact with both generations. The night before, she had gone to the opening day of the large nearby amusement park with the younger generation. Today she was functioning as the mother of a ten-year-old daughter and the head of a household that included her two children, her own younger brother, and her mother. Dee Dee's mother was an active Muslim who wore floor-length dresses and kept her head and arms and body covered with modest and loose-fitting clothing. She did not interact with any neighbors or other individuals on the block.

Dee Dee, on the other hand, was one of the most sociable people on the block. When the recently formed block association decided to put on a block party for the children this past summer, Dee Dee was active in planning, shopping, and the work of the event itself. One of Dee Dee's favorite spots was her second-floor front window, from which she would watch the activities on the street below. Unlike her modest and proper mother, Dee Dee was most likely during these hours of watching to wear a bathrobe.

It was from this window perch that Dee Dee saw the public part of the family fight that led Clara to take up residence with the Wards. Clara's mother, a preacher at a church located in a nearby community, did not become involved in the street part of the family squabble. But Clara's father, a hip man-about-town in his own estimation, and her drug-addicted older brother were both trying to suppress Clara's assertions of independence. Clara's feeling of independence had been growing since she spent time as part of a Job Corps group in a neighboring state.

Clara was now adding some of her experiences in the Job Corps to the discussion about health care that Gloria and Dee Dee were carrying on in the Ward kitchen. Even Gert became involved when the talk got around to her own stay in the Jewish hospital during an operation on her leg. Except for the early pain in her leg, Gert had had an enjoyable time visiting with her friends and listening to the stories of how they had lied about their ages in order to be able to go up and see her in the hospital. Gert also remembered enjoying the fried chicken, greens, and potato salad her friends had smuggled up to her to offset the skimpy kosher meals served by the hospital.

At that time Gert's hospital stay had been made possible by her father's job-connected insurance. Gloria had never used that coverage for herself, but she was glad it was available to take care of the children.

There were two other hospitals available to pregnant women, and neither Gert nor Ann had decided which to use. One was a Protestant church-connected institution on the northern border of Blackston. Although it was much smaller than either the Jewish hospital or the County Hospital, some women from the block who had given birth there recommended it highly. They felt it had concerned doctors, many of whom were foreigners, a warmer atmosphere, which they associated with the small size of the institution, and more flexible rules, especially as concerned mother-infant interaction. The County Hospital was considered by many, not only the patients from this area but also some of the staff of other hospitals, to have a superior department of pediatrics and maternity. But the size of the hospital worked against any personal doctor-patient relationships and against flexibility in applying rules. In addition, the distance of the hospital from Blackston affected the ease with which family and friends could visit. Both Gert and Little Ann were more interested in this latter consideration, since they expected no medical complications.

Dee Dee was arguing in favor of the Jewish hospital, but Clara pointed out that the local community council had recently boycotted it. A Black baby and a Spanish baby had been allowed to die in the emergency room through medical neglect, the council said. All of the women became involved in the argument, and Ann returned from the living room to join in too.

During all this, Gloria continued cooking in the several pots on the stove top. The oven door remained open in an attempt to heat the house, since it was midway between the periods when heat was turned on. The thirteen-year-old family cat climbed up onto the washing machine that was fitted in tight against the kitchen sink. The dogs were tied to the bathroom door and dozing in front of the apartment door they were supposed to protect. Brenda's daughter, Bobby, was watching TV and keeping her eye on her half sisters, the infant twins, and on Donald, Little Ann's small son. When Brenda returned from work, Bobby and the twins would go back upstairs to their own apartment. During all of this, Oscar continued to sleep in the back room.

WHEN OSCAR WOKE UP and came out into the kitchen, the group had changed somewhat. Dee Dee had gone back into her own apartment across the hall. Oscar wished she'd spend more time there and less in his kitchen. His youngest daughter had gone to the corner store for Aunt Bea. And Val, Naomi's godfather, had come to visit. Already Gloria had set a big plate full of food in front of Val. If anyone ever left the Ward home hungry, it wouldn't be Gloria's fault.

Oscar said he wasn't hungry. But his presleep thoughts had put him in the mood to reminisce. He did this by reminding Val of the occasion a couple of years earlier when Naomi had become their godchild. At that time Oscar and his family still lived on the first floor of the two-family house across the street. The six rooms had meant more space for the family, but even so, the apartment hadn't seemed large enough. There had been a bad spell of illnesses and other expenses in the family, so that Gloria fell more and more behind in the mortgage payments, and the upstairs tenant had failed to pay the money he promised. They had had to move when their overdue payments amounted to more than they could catch up with. At that time Val and his wife had been living in the first-floor rear apartment next door. They offered to hold the christening party in their apartment because the boiler had broken down in the Wards' house and no money was available to make the extensive repairs required.

Oscar remembered the christening party very well. Naomi seemed so tiny then. The presents she received from family and friends were piled almost as high as she stood. Oscar had contributed a two-pound jar of caviar from the specialty-foods company he worked for. Oscar didn't like caviar. And from what Bettylou told him after the party, no one else did either. She and Jack from across the street had spent several evenings doing various things with the leftover caviar. Sour cream hadn't helped, and when Hank and Jack decided to mix it into a biscuit batter, everyone insisted that the entire mixture be thrown out. Oscar knew from his job that caviar was an expensive item, and he had

wanted to contribute something important to the party. So as far
as he was concerned, the father had done his part.

Naomi's mother had arranged the church-related part of the
christening. Although Gloria's own uncle was the minister in a
church on Stanner Avenue, in another section of Blackston, she
decided to call on "Bishop" Wells to do the christening. Bishop
Wells was a community figure of long standing. At one time he
had organized a "cadet corps" and band with help from the local
War on Poverty agency. Gloria's son Edward had been a member
of both. Whenever Bishop Wells was in the neighborhood, he
would stop at the Wards' home. No one in the Ward family attended any church regularly or even irregularly. But they kept up
church ties for ceremonial occasions such as christenings, wed-
dings, and funerals.

Oscar remembered attending prayer meetings in his living
room. It had come about this way. It was summer. The family
was sitting on the front steps when they were approached by a
man who explained that he was leader of a storefront mission in
another district. He said he was walking through the Blackston
area and felt that people needed help. He also wanted to increase
his mission membership by working here on this block. Gloria
agreed to hold a prayer meeting once a week on Wednesday night
at the Ward house. Wednesday was chosen because many of the
people who might attend would be busy on weekend nights with
card games or parties, and the minister wanted the weekend to
prepare his Sunday morning service at the mission.

The meetings had gone on for about two months. Oscar recalled only two things from those prayer meetings. One was that
his drinking was frequently the most discussed item, and the second was that the most often repeated prayer was that he stop
drinking the devil's brew. In the ecstasy and excitement of the
meeting, Oscar sometimes promised to do so. But the next week
always required new prayers that the Lord again forgive his continued drinking. Drinking or not, praying or not, Oscar was
always able to keep up with his work schedule and bring home
the weekly paycheck. He would remind himself of this when he
felt especially bad about drinking.

Bettylou, who had recently moved to this area to do a study,
came to each meeting at Gloria's invitation. The second thing

that Oscar remembered from these prayer meetings was related to Bettylou. Oscar had seen but not heard the incident. It was only later, when Gloria and Bettylou told the story to others, that Oscar understood what everyone was smiling about. After one of the prayer meetings the Reverend Tomes had taken Bettylou's hand in both of his and gazed into her eyes while Mrs. Tomes continued playing "Nearer my God to Thee" on the Wards' out-of-tune piano. Still holding her hand the Reverend murmured, "My dear, I believe God has great things in store for you."

Oscar's tendency to ramble and reinspect earlier, happier times was brought to an end by Val's asking him to come across the street and help with a block-association project of repairing a fence. The fence was needed to keep garbage out of the vacant, block-long lot behind Oscar's old house. The vacant lot had resulted when all the homes and buildings on the next street across from the railroad tracks had been torn down as part of urban renewal. The various houses had been taken down by different contractors at different times, as they became city property through abandonment, years of nonpayment of taxes by the absentee landlords, or other neglect. The flimsy fences required by law around all razed property did not connect with each other. In addition, one fence had often fallen down before the next-door one was built. Some fences were even torn down by a later contractor who saved money by using the old fence on his present job. The fence only had to last until the city inspector came to approve the demolition job a few weeks later. What happened after that was of no interest to the contractor or to the city.

After all the houses that backed on this block had been torn down, the sanitation department had decided to use the street as a dumping place for all the garbage trucks servicing this section of Blackston. When the block association had complained to the health department and the city administration, the sanitation department had argued that all the garbage dumped in that area was removed by the end of each day. One city department convinced the other that dumping garbage on a city street, a half block from occupied dwellings, was necessary because it was too expensive and time-consuming for the sanitation trucks to go all the way to the official city dump far from Blackston. The residents on the street knew that the garbage remained for many nights and attracted rats as well as private dumpers, who added their loads to the city's garbage piles and thus avoided the fees charged to private commercial users of the city dump. The block association took photographs of the illegal dumping, called and reported violators to the city bureau that licensed them, and tried to enlist the support of the newly formed Model Cities agency in Blackston. All of this brought no change.

Oscar was aware of the problem, and so were most of his age mates and drinking buddies on the block. But they were very cynical about fighting the city and didn't offer to help. Many of their wives were active in the block association, so they knew about all the efforts that didn't seem to bring any success. A few of the men on the block voiced their belief that it would be a waste of time to try to do anything. Although Oscar said he agreed with them, he couldn't refuse to help Val when asked directly.

Oscar got up to put on a warm jacket and made Val promise to bring back his copies of the christening-party pictures so they could continue talking about it. Although the Wards had a set of the same pictures, it was always a major job to find them among the clutter of such crowded living. After working a while on the fence, Oscar planned to try to get Val to buy a pint of whiskey too. But he didn't mention this aloud while his wife was with them in the kitchen. With mixed motives, Val and Oscar went out to fight city hall.

In the meantime, Gloria had finished most of the cooking for the day. She decided to go downstairs and talk with her sister Bea about their tentative plans to visit their father in a town several hours' drive away.

The food, which on this midweek day included roast pork, green beans, sweet potatoes, and biscuits, would be left on the stove to simmer or on the open oven door to keep warm. Each family member would eat when she or he got hungry. The older children would serve the younger ones. And sometimes three or four people might sit down together to eat.

Most of the time there was no formally agreed-upon or scheduled time to eat. On special occasions, such as Thanksgiving or some other holiday, a birthday, or a visit from special friends or family members from outside of Blackston, Gloria would put on a

dinner party that sometimes sat as many as sixteen people in this
combination kitchen/dining room. Such a dinner usually meant
that the weekly paycheck went totally for food. There would be
no payment of bills, no buying of clothes, no dry cleaning, no
household items that week. After the leftover food was finished, it
might even mean no food, or they would have to borrow to just
get by. Everyone knew this and seemed to accept it as the price of
a celebration, in the same way that no one seemed to mind being
squeezed up close to the refrigerator, washing machine, dish
cabinet, or stove at such a dinner. Attention was focused on being
with one another and on cooking and eating.

One Thanksgiving dinner started with grapefruit halves and
shrimp cocktail and featured turkey, chicken, ham, and roast
beef. These were accompanied by the traditional Thanksgiving
cranberries, corn, sweet potatoes, and mashed potatoes, as well
as the usual collard greens, blackeye peas, and rice with gravy.
For dessert there were cakes and pies prepared by Gloria the
night before and during the early morning hours. Most of the dinner guests on this occasion were immediate family or aunts,
uncles, cousins, and mates of these family members. The few
nonfamily guests had arrived at the appointed time and entered a
scene of ongoing cooking. They waited for nearly four hours for
all the dinner items to be completed before eating.

Cooking was something that everyone in this household, male
and female, learned to do, usually without very explicit direction
or urging. Some family members specialized in certain items. For
instance, Edward, who had spent some time in trade school
learning to be a baker, preferred to work on baked goods. Often
he and his sister Ann argued about who could, and how to, make
the best lemon meringue pie. Oscar, the father, tended to cook
one-pot mixtures that often included meat, vegetables, and rice
or dumplings. Sometimes a particular youngster would be asked
to fix something or keep an eye on a given pot. At other times
several people in turn might stir, taste, comment on, or add to
some cooking item.

Gloria was glad to leave her own stove and go down to sit and
talk with Bea. They usually managed to get together at least once
each day. Bea might be cooking too. Or, if she had decided to
drink rather than cook, Gloria would send down a big plateful of

food later. Bea's cooking tended to be more mainstream American or even ethnic Jewish than Gloria's, probably because of the differences in their past employment. Gloria had worked outside of her home on occasion when it became necessary to supplement Oscar's paycheck. But most of the time her family of seven had required that she spend time at home.

Bea, on the other hand, had only one grown son, had long been a widow, and was currently unmarried and living alone. She had spent large periods of time in the employ of suburban householders; often as a cook or as an all-round domestic worker. Bea had thus learned the food preferences, cooking styles, and customs of her employers and prided herself on being able to cook in a variety of styles. During this same time, the families for whom she worked, especially the children, learned about items common in Blackston and similar communities, such as grits and greens.

When Gloria walked into Bea's small apartment, she didn't see or smell anything cooking. Bea seemed very glad to see Gloria and opened up the conversation by telling her sister how she had thrown Oscar out of her house earlier that day. This was a scene often enacted and reenacted between the two sisters. Bea had been very critical of Oscar when her sister had first brought him around during the Second World War. And now, twenty-five years later, Bea still felt the same way. Gloria, in turn, seemed to agree with all Bea's complaints, and an outsider might wonder why she remained married to Oscar. Oscar, for his part, wasn't there to hear today's complaints, but he had heard them many times in the past. He seemed able to live with the complaints, however unhappily, and to keep functioning as wage earner for his wife and children.

Part of the reason the two women agreed on this topic was probably related to their joint background. Their own upbringing had been in a solidly respectable northern town rather than a big-city ghetto area. Their father had come to the United States from the Caribbean, and although his grandchildren and great-grandchildren considered themselves just Black, Bea and Gloria still held to their Caribbean origins and background and expressed them to others. Each would make explicit if asked or challenged their belief that West Indians were smarter, harder-working, better-mannered, and otherwise superior to American colored people.

Oscar with his poor, southern country background, had always been treated like a country bumpkin by Bea. And although Gloria had gone ahead with her plans to marry Oscar and had lived with him for twenty-five years, she didn't often defend Oscar publicly or in private to Bea.

Bea began to tell Gloria her latest news of Roland, Bea's only son. Roland had been born when Bea was quite young, and much of his upbringing had not been in Bea's hands. Now Roland was a good-looking, fortyish Black man living in a middle-class Black suburb some miles from Blackston. He occasionally came to Blackston, sometimes in his sports car or on his elaborate motorcycle, to visit briefly with Bea and other family members who happened to be around, and quickly went off again. Bea didn't like Roland to find her drinking, but she wanted the visits, which were almost always unannounced and unpredictable. Even this problem was better than the many years during which Roland refused to have any contact with his mother. Bea knew that during that period he had been seeing a psychiatrist, but she never did learn from Roland whether this was related to his decision to get back in touch with her.

Today's news was about an invitation for Bea to spend Mother's Day with Roland and his wife and son at their suburban home. Bea was excited and proud. She had already begun to make plans about what to wear and was asking Gloria to fix her hair in a special style.

Gloria was the hairdresser in the Ward family. Most of her teenage and young-adult daughters had recently begun to wear their hair in the Afro style that was becoming popular among their friends. Neither Gloria nor Bea was very happy about the Afro style and preferred to continue pressing and curling their own relatively "good" hair. Before the Afro became popular, Gloria had spent part of most days helping one or another of her daughters, their friends, and later their grandchildren to press (with a hot comb), braid, curl, or style their hair. Often this was done in the kitchen and served as a focus of activity for an afternoon. Just last weekend Gloria had done Bettylou's hair for a party while she sat and talked with Gert and Brenda about their school experiences.

Bea didn't want to talk or think about anyone else just now. She wanted only to plan for the upcoming Mother's Day trip. She began talking about possible presents she might take to her son's wife, Eileen. Eileen had been a high-school sweetheart of Roland's. She had called Bea "Mother" then and told her that the one thing in life she had determined would happen was that she would marry Roland. The two of them had been married now for almost eighteen years, and their only son, Justin, was a six-foot-tall teenage chess fan and high-school sports hero.

Bea had the money to spend on a gift now, since she had been working steadily for the past ten weeks for the dentist's wife who had been her employer in spells for the past five or six years. When Bea wasn't working for the dentist's wife, she was often working for the same woman's sister-in-law, who was married to a doctor. Sometimes Bea worked two or three days for each of them at the same time. At times like this she provided a common background for the small cousins in her charge and helped the sisters exchange gossip. In addition Bea did the cleaning, shopping, cooking, and babysitting. Both the doctor and the dentist had been promising to provide professional services to Bea at no cost or only at the cost of materials. So far neither had done anything, so Bea, like her sister Gloria, remained overweight and lacking a front tooth or two.

Before Bea had gone back to work for the dentist's wife, she had a half year of subsisting on a welfare check of $17 per week and about $25 more per week that she earned illegally by caring for the two small children of a working mother who lived in the city-owned apartment building across the street and for the small child of the anthropologists. She charged them $3 or $4 per day to provide three meals, constant attention, game playing, reading stories, or just watching the children while they sat or stood on the stoop during the warm weather. In addition, Bea would sometimes agree to watch the infants or toddlers of her kin, even though this usually did not involve any cash payment. Bea often said that she loved children and wished she had had more. But she always added, "God didn't bless me with any more children, and that's why with everybody else's child I try to do nice things."

During this period Bea had been able to fulfill her food needs and provide some household necessities, but she never had much to spend for other things. She was able to pay her rent because the

West Indian landlord in her building and the Jewish couple who owned the tenement next door paid her a small amount each month to keep the halls clean in both buildings, to see that the front stoop was swept and that the garbage cans lined up on the sidewalk in front of the buildings were kept neat.

Bea was able to keep up with these chores, plus the 7 A.M. to 6 or 7 P.M. babysitting, by hiring Randy, the addict from up the street, to mop the hallways. Bea herself swept off the stoops early each morning. There was very little anyone could do about the garbage cans, many of which were battered by the garbage men as they threw them around. Some of the cans were losing or had lost their bottoms or lids, and there were too few to hold all the garbage produced by the large families in the six tenement apartments at both houses.

During the ten weeks of working for the dentist's wife, Bea hadn't been drinking at all. Today was the first day in several months of returning to alcohol. This was part of a pattern Bea had developed. For weeks or months at a time she would not drink at all. During these times she became very insistent upon "proper" behavior from her kin and friends—no swearing, respect for elders, moderate or no drinking, set mealtimes, modest clothing, and other customs less honored during Bea's drinking periods.

But Bea's values weren't merely anchored to her drinking habits. Gloria reminded her today about the dinner party Bea had given for Gloria and Oscar's wedding anniversary. The guests had included the Wards, Bernice and Hank, Val and Bettylou, and various of the Ward children and teenagers, who came and went. All the adults, including Bea, had been drinking for some time before dinner was served. Everyone was seated at Bea's food-laden table when Randy and some other addicts knocked at the door. They had sacks of potatoes and onions and several cartons of canned foods taken from the freight cars on the siding nearby. Bea had immediately tried to send them away, saying that it was illegal and not right to be taking someone else's food and she wouldn't have them selling it in her apartment. But both Gloria and Bernice had gone out to the door, looked over the offering, and argued a little about price, and finally each had bought a sack of potatoes, a sack of onions, and various cans of

food. The entire transaction had taken place in the hallway outside Bea's door with only the light from her kitchen to provide a
little illumination.

Gloria called upstairs and had her son Edward come to carry
her purchases up to their apartment. Bernice asked Hank to take
hers across to their house. Bea allowed that, in order not to break
up the dinner party further, Bernice could just leave the things inside the kitchen door and take them home later. Although Bea
was willing to give in to expediency on that issue, she was very active in arguing that all this behavior was wrong. Bea pointed out,
as everyone already knew, that Randy and his friends had stolen
the items from the railroad. It was Hank who pointed out that
stealing from the railroad wasn't like stealing from an individual
in that the materials were probably already counted as an expected loss and/or completely covered by insurance. His wife Bernice agreed strongly. Gloria expressed the view that she couldn't
possibly feed all her family each week and provide everything else
that was needed on Oscar's paycheck, so she needed bargains like
this to make ends meet. The Valentines took no active part in this
conversation, so Bea was left arguing in a heartfelt and morally
indignant way against the buying of stolen goods while her kin
and friends defended it as fair in the circumstances and the only
way to get a reasonable deal in the ghetto. Bea made the point,
and Gloria agreed, that they had never taught the Ward children
to steal; in fact they had been taught not to steal. But although
Bea felt this point supported her argument, Gloria countered that
it was only her own children for whom she was responsible and
over whom she had any control. The morality, need for, and
meaning of the transaction had been the main item of conversation during the entire dinner.

Bea didn't especially want to be reminded of the event. She still
felt that she had been right but had not prevailed. But her main
interest now was not in that question but in her plans for the upcoming Mother's Day dinner at her son's home. He was to come
and pick Bea up in the late morning, and she was to spend the entire day with his family. Bea went on at some length about how
wonderful her son, daughter-in-law, and grandchild were to do
this for her.

During Bea's talk about Roland, she was interrupted several

times by various of Gloria's children putting their heads in at Bea's unlocked door to ask their mother some question, or calling down from the steps between the two apartments. Gloria would answer or step momentarily out of the room to find something or settle a problem. Bea finally told Gloria that she didn't like trying to hold a serious conversation with her because Gloria couldn't sit still long enough. Bea, who could be very indulgent with children, often felt that Gloria was too indulgent with hers.

Gloria was used to this complaint. She never really tried to stop the interruptions, or at least her efforts weren't taken seriously by the children. It all made Gloria feel needed. For years she had been having chest pains, and when she finally went to see a doctor, who suggested that she go into the hospital for tests, Gloria refused. Her stated reason was that the house would fall apart without her presence as organizer, peacemaker, and focus. Only she knew the secrets and bargains necessary to make Oscar's check cover their expenses, and only she could keep after him to get free items like day-old bread from places where he made deliveries. Besides, as she pointed out in defending her refusal, Oscar's insurance coverage wouldn't pay for diagnostic work, as they had found when their daughter Gert had trouble with her leg. And they had no savings at all.

Gloria believed in preventive medicine, particularly for babies and children. She had fed her children vitamins, taken them to the well-baby clinic or a private doctor, and dealt immediately with any symptoms of illness. Yet all of this was for her children, nieces, nephews, and grandchildren. Gloria, who was following out her own line of thought, told Bea that for adults who had to be at home or at work each day there was neither the time nor the money for illness. Therefore many adults refused to think about their aches and pains and hoped that most physical problems would clear up without care. Bea didn't always agree, but she knew that Gloria would find many older people in Blackston who felt this way. Bea herself had gone to the doctor when she began to have pains in her hands, only to be told that there was nothing to be done about it except take aspirin when it hurt too much. Gloria had scoffed at this waste of money for a doctor's visit and told Bea that she could have prescribed aspirin. Besides, as they both knew, everyone hurt more as they grew older, and Bea and

Gloria knew many such people in this community who made their own pains secondary to other immediate needs such as employment, child care, cooking, and similar duties. Oscar tended to agree with Gloria, but he worried about his wife's chest pains and dizziness. Yet on those few occasions when he insisted that he could run the household as well as work, Gloria dismissed the entire discussion.

Bea, on the other hand, who had no family obligations around which to focus her life, often warned her sister to take care of her health, stating that if Gloria didn't, she might soon be away from her family permanently. The two sisters obviously had a long-standing and ongoing relationship in which they criticized and supported each other. Today Bea continued drinking even though her sister Gloria wouldn't join her. Gloria drank only at parties or on special occasions.

This session was finally broken up totally by Naomi's return from the store, where she had gone for Aunt Bea. Gloria and Naomi returned upstairs to their own apartment to eat, and it was only on the way upstairs that Gloria remembered her earlier intention to talk with Bea about visiting their father. Oh well, she could see Bea later tonight or tomorrow. Bea, who had been drinking most of the day, began to feel lonely when she was left by herself in the apartment. She felt depressed and unhappy with her life. Bea recognized this feeling as a familiar one and knew that if she didn't do something about it she would be unable to sleep and would probably feel a need to begin the next day with a drink too.

Bea decided to go across the street to talk with Val and Betty-lou. She had done so before. Both her father and her son had encouraged her to continue to do so if it made her feel better. Bea knew that she couldn't have an uninterrupted talk with Gloria. Gloria might just respond jokingly and not understand the emotional significance of Bea's feelings. Occasionally, as Bea now reminded herself, she had tried to talk with Roland. He had been mostly sympathetic, but he didn't like to be awakened by the phone in the late night or early morning, and this was often when Bea needed help most. In addition, there were some things Bea felt she couldn't discuss with her son.

When Bea knocked at the Valentines' door, both Val and

Bettylou were at home. Their son, Jonathan, whom Bea often cared for, was asleep. Val had just recently parted company with Oscar after some post-fence-building drinks. Bettylou was gathering together the christening pictures she had promised to take over to the Wards' the next day. Bea asked the two of them to listen to her troubles, saying that she felt her drinking problems might get out of hand if she didn't deal with her problems first. The Valentines said they would and asked Bea if she would feel comfortable if a tape recorder was recording in the background. Bea agreed, telling the Valentines that she loved them, was sure they loved her and would not embarrass her or hurt her.

Bea was happy with the fact that she was able to talk uninterruptedly for as long as she wanted. She talked about her childhood, her father, her mother, and her grandmother, with whom she had lived for some time. Mostly she seemed to want to talk about her marriage, her husband's death, her fear and depression thereafter, and finally her present, deeply felt need for affection. She talked about all the children she enjoyed taking care of and repeated aloud for others what she had known for a long time—that her days were bearable if she had a lot of work, children to care for, and companions, but the nights, when she had to be by herself, were terrible. Bea talked about living in with the family she did housework for, as they had asked, but felt she would miss the neighborhood and her relatives. Besides, she did not see this as a solution to her problem, which she felt was in her head. It would also keep her from finding the social and sexual company of a man.

Val and Bettylou listened sympathetically and didn't comment until Bea said she felt talked out. Then they suggested that Bea's account indicated to them that she needed a "companion" and should regard even very strong desires for this as quite normal.

Bea didn't talk any more but she felt less depressed and left saying she thought she might sleep now.

EDWARD, OSCAR'S SECOND SON and namesake, was spending his day with his older brother Raymond. They had always been close and enjoyed many of the same things—mostly jazz and the musical groups they had put together and played in. Today Edward and Raymond talked about what to do with the audio-phono equipment that represented the bulk of their salaries. Raymond was about to be sent overseas, and the current group would probably break up. Edward wanted to keep the amplifiers but didn't know where. Although his mate, Little Ann, lived at his parents' home and Edward himself sometimes slept there, he knew that he didn't want to keep his fancy equipment in such a crowded place with so many people, including small children, who might mess with it.

Raymond suggested that Milford might agree to keep it and let Edward use it at his parents' house, where he was furnishing and decorating his own basement rooms. Milford was a family friend whose parents were from South America. Milford's older brother, Richard, who played with the band, was married to the Wards' oldest daughter, Brenda, and Milford himself was dating their sister Ann. Edward liked the idea of using Milford's place, and his reasons weren't all musical. If the equipment was in Milford's basement rooms, Edward would have an excuse to see Milford's younger sister more often. Although Little Ann was now pregnant with Edward's second child, he felt fairly sure he didn't want to remain with her. He did want the children, though, and so did his mother, Gloria, who encouraged Little Ann and her son Donald to stay in the Ward apartment. Edward planned to stay at his job at the same plant where his father worked and to help support Donald; his mother would see to that. If he didn't, the money would have to come from Gloria and her family, and she couldn't afford to do this on Oscar's salary. It was hard to know whether Little Ann would share the welfare check she received for Donald with Mrs. Ward or not. It might well depend on how the relationship between Edward and Little Ann ended. No matter about that, Edward knew he had no plans to marry Little Ann.

That was a subject he'd rather not think about. Unknowingly Raymond saved him from doing so by talking about the engagements the band had played, many at the nearby army base where Raymond had been stationed these past three years. Edward joined with him in recalling some of those occasions, including the time the man in charge of the club at the base had tried to slip away one Saturday night while the band was still

playing, to avoid paying them. Despite things like that from people of higher rank, Raymond was generally pleased with his work
and friends at the base. This was one of the reasons he signed up
for a second term. He was promised that he'd be retained at his
job of recruiting young Black men for the Vietnam War. Now
here he was being shipped to Thailand himself, and there seemed
to be no way to change the orders.

In addition to breaking up the band, these orders to go overseas
had forced Raymond to make a decision about getting married.
He had been thinking about it and had been going with Susan for
some time. But when Raymond was ordered overseas, they had
both decided to be married right away. Now they were having a
hard time finding a place where Susan could live. She might have
to stay with her parents across the street in the rehabilitated
building for a while, since Raymond's home had been in Aunt
Bea's third room during his posting to the nearby army base, and
that space was barely big enough for a bed, a dresser, and the
audio-phono equipment. Anyway, Aunt Bea and Susan weren't
close enough friends to stay in the same apartment without Raymond around.

Raymond and Edward decided to catch a service car and go
over to Milford's house to talk about keeping the equipment
there. Although both men knew how to drive, there hadn't been
anything in the Ward family to drive since Oscar's ancient Buick
had broken down for the millionth time. Sometimes Edward
tried working on it, sometimes Oscar fiddled around with it while
his friend Rob drove around helping to search for spare parts at
the various junkyards close by. Until a short time ago the car just
sat at the curb and was used by the older men when they wanted
to sit and talk and drink together, away but not far away from
their homes and women.

The service car carrying Raymond and Edward entered the
mixed Latin-Black-White community some miles from Blackston
where Milford lived. Milford's family had moved here less than a
year ago from the house on Paul Street where the Wards still
lived. Milford's family had been among the first non-Whites to
move onto Paul Street in the late 1950s. For the past dozen years
they had been paying the mortgage off on a two-family brick
house on Paul Street. They lived on the first floor, made the base-

ment into a separate apartment, and rented rooms on the second floor to their countrymen. During the time they had been buying, altering, and improving the house, they paid for fire insurance from a private company through the bank as mortgagor. Within two weeks after they had made the last mortgage payment and become the sole owners of the house, the insurance company that had covered them for twelve years for the bank refused to continue coverage. Milford's parents expressed their anger at this discrimination to anyone who would listen and tried in various ways to secure fire insurance from other sources, but none was available for a privately owned house in an area like Blackston. They sold the house, losing much of the money and the twelve years of work and materials that had gone into improving the property, because they felt they had no alternative. Milford's father pointed out that they couldn't remain in an area with such a high fire rate without fire insurance or they might lose their total investment and all their belongings. So they moved to a new neighborhood that seemed a little nicer and began again the whole process that was part of the American dream of owning a house.

Raymond and Edward weren't generally interested in the insurance question or anything else that did not directly affect them. But they did know about automobile insurance. In fact the high cost of auto insurance was one of the reasons they didn't put more time and effort into fixing their father's car. And they had both talked about car insurance with the Valentines, who had given Edward his first driving lesson. They were not as surprised or angry as the Valentines were to hear that in addition to charging high rates for collision coverage to anyone listing a Blackston address, the Valentines' insurance company of many yejrs' standing refused to provide any comprehensive coverage while they lived and worked in Blackston. During this same discussion, the Valentines had talked with Edward about the possibility that he was less shocked by such discrimination on the part of institutions because, unlike themselves, he had never experienced any different treatment. Edward remembered pointing out that he had had many experiences outside of Blackston. He had gone to a technical school in a different part of the city and traveled with the band to different areas and even spent some time in the homes and neighborhoods of his mother's employers. Edward argued that it was not a lack of knowledge that kept him from being angry but the sure knowledge that he couldn't do anything about it.

They both began to deal with the immediate problem of paying the service-car driver, who had just pulled up on Milford's street. Edward insisted that he had to keep his money because he'd already arranged to buy some smoke for all of them that evening from a friend's friend, and besides, Raymond was getting steady pay from the army. Edward, who had spent the minimum term in the navy and was generally not happy with the choice of employer he had made, slightly resented the easier time Raymond seemed to have in the army. Edward settled the argument by walking away to ring Milford's doorbell, leaving Raymond to pay the driver. He didn't give him a tip. This was usual practice in Blackston, particularly among welfare residents and younger people, who usually had less money to spend, assumed that the driver had already included his tip in the unmetered price he was quoting, and thought of tips as alien to the ghetto.

Edward and Raymond didn't worry about whether they had fare to return to Blackston. They would try to borrow it if necessary. Or they might both spend the night at Milford's, depending on what was going on that evening and where they were expected to be in the morning. There always seemed to be some chair or couch to put up one more person and always enough food for visitors. If the night was interesting, people might not sleep at all or might just nap. For all these reasons it wasn't always easy to be clear about where a young male "lived." This was much less true for females, though. Gert, who was in the same age group as Edward, could be more accurately described as living at home.

She was certainly at home now. Gert's pregnancy made her large, uncomfortable, and not eager to move about. She had agreed to stay at the house and mind Donald while her mother, sister, and Little Ann went on a shopping trip to the main commercial area in Blackston. They would probably walk the dozen blocks to reach the area and take a service car on the return trip, when they had packages to carry. This hmlped to save money. Gloria had spent most of Oscar's weekly check on Saturday stocking up on groceries, but she wanted to use what was left to buy

some clothes for Naomi. Naomi was growing faster than any of
Gloria's children. Just nearing her eleventh year, she was already
5′5″and weighed 150 pounds. Her older sisters wouldn't let her
borrow their clothes any more.

Naomi was not doing well in school, although this seemed to
improve when Gloria and the teacher both worked with her. But
this year Naomi had a teacher who dismissed her from finishing
her work and instead had Naomi comb, brush, and otherwise
tend the teacher's hair during class. Gloria had found this out by
accident and confirmed it through several of the other children
before going to the school to protest. The teacher had not denied
the activity; she had merely said that Naomi would not concen-
trate on her school work and obviously enjoyed doing something
that interested her and at which she was good. So the public
school system, through Naomi's fifth-grade teacher, indulged her
talent for doing hair rather than teaching her to read and write.
Gloria hoped for a better sixth-grade teacher—someone she could
work with.

Gert was staring at a TV game show when she heard Aunt Bea
call from the bottom of the stairs. She smacked the dog tied to the
apartment door and told him to shut up as she stuck her head out
to call back. Aunt Bea insisted that Gert come down, saying she
didn't want to carry on her business in the hall. Gert and Aunt
Bea were on neutral terms just now. Sometimes they were more
friendly, sometimes less so. Some time ago, when the Wards lived
across the street, Gloria and Bea had worked out an arrangement
for Gert to move in with her aunt, so as to provide Bea with company and a little household help. Gert, for her part, was to get a
quiet and more orderly place in which to do her school work. The
arrangement had not lasted long. Gert had found Aunt Bea too
bossy, and Aunt Bea refused to put up with what she considered
unhelpful, ungrateful, and sassy behavior.

Gert slipped into her old shoes, which served as slippers since
she had bent down the backs of the shoes, and flopped loudly on
each step as she went down to Bea's. She had picked Donald up
and carried him down with her despite his protests. Gert knocked
on Bea's door and walked into the kitchen immediately without
waiting for the "come in" shouted from the front room. The door
to Raymond's room was shut, as it always was when he wasn't
there. Earlier, when Gert had lived with Aunt Bea, she had

shared what was now Raymond's room with Bea. Now Aunt Bea slept in the living room on a sofabed.

Aunt Bea was not sure when Raymond would be back, if at all, that night. She was often asleep when he came in. She would leave food for him on the stove. But she knew that Gert might see him, since the young people all seemed to keep late hours, or Raymond might call on the phone at the Ward apartment. Bea, like many Blackston residents, didn't have a telephone. The Wards had one now because Little Ann had worked briefly for the phone company and was not required to make a deposit before installation as were all other Blackstonians, in contrast with people from wealthier sections of the city. If Raymond called, Bea had a message that had to be acted on right away. The West Indian family in the third-floor front apartment in this building had decided to move into the area across from Blackston's southwest border. This area was a lower-middle-class community whose Jewish population was moving out and being replaced by West Indians, other Blacks, and some Hispanics—as had happened in Blackston a dozen years earlier.

The landlord had told Aunt Bea about the move and asked if she knew of anyone who would be interested in taking the apartment. He didn't want anyone on welfare. Bea immediately thought of Raymond and Susan.

If Raymond and Susan decided to take the place, Susan would be close to her in-laws and the rest of the Ward extended family. Brenda and Richard lived with Bobby and the twins in the third-floor rear apartment; Gloria, Oscar, and their remaining children in the second-floor rear; and Aunt Bea in the first-floor front. In addition, Susan would be able to remain close to her parents and among established friends and neighbors while Raymond was in Thailand.

Gert liked the idea too because for her it would mean the company of someone near her age and a place to go when she got tired of her family's crowded and often noisy home. Gert knew she would receive some payment for her expected child from the welfare department. In fact she had already received a check to buy clothes and materials. But because she was under eighteen she would be discouraged from setting up an apartment or home separate from her parents. Gert wasn't sure she wanted to do that anyway. She expected almost without conscious thought that her mother would help care for her baby and leave Gert free to party and socialize away from home like other seventeen-year-olds. Her mother's doting treatment of Donald contradicted her occasional statements to Gert that she wasn't going to take care of any more babies.

Gert had neither planned for nor against a baby. She was very uncertain about whether she wanted to marry the baby's father. In fact, she had told her mother and others that she didn't want to be married to anyone just now. Her sister Brenda didn't get married until Bobby was nearly five years old, and she had done well. Brenda had kept up a job with the insurance company, bought nice clothes, and had an apartment of her own before she ever got married to Richard. From Gert's point of view marriage was no big thing.

Gert knew she couldn't say this sort of thing to Aunt Bea, so she didn't try. Instead she agreed to deliver the message to Raymond and urge him to do something definite the next day. The landlord had told Bea that the West Indian family expected to move out Wednesday and she could have the key to the apartment then. Aunt Bea often collected rents from the tenants as part of her work for the landlord.

Aunt Bea and the West Indian family had been quite friendly during the few months they had lived on the block. Bea had often taken care of their two school-age boys after school, before their father had returned from his daytime job as a security guard downtown and after their mother had left for her night shift of private-duty nursing. Aunt Bea expected that they would tell her about their new home in the next day or two, but like many people in Blackston they probably would not let many others know. It always seemed safer to keep your business to yourself, especially if it involved property or changes related to income or residence. Yet Bea was aware, from having lived on Paul Street for over eight years, that many of the people who moved away in what seemed a day without word to friends were often back within a week or a month to keep up old social ties. Even people like Thaddeus across the way, who often spoke of hating this neighborhood, had admitted to Bea in early-morning conversations with her as she sat in her street-level window seat that this area was a community, a place of friends and ties that made for more than just neighbors in an impersonal, big-city setting. Aunt Bea was aware of the many former residents who came back to visit, party, or perhaps play cards on a Saturday night in someone's home or at one of the informal social clubs on the street.

Bea went back to her window seat and Gert trudged back upstairs, where she had left the apartment door unlocked. The dog, who was continually tied to the door, had pulled it open trying to get out. Usually if an apartment was empty it would not be left unlocked. But this was one of the safest buildings on the block, except for the first-floor rear apartment, which backed on-to an unused alleyway. It was safe because Aunt Bea kept an almost constant watch from her first-floor window on everyone entering the building, and she had come to know all of the friends, neighbors, and acquaintances of everyone in the building. Aunt Bea saw most of what happened on the street from her window.

She was there only a few feet from him when Oscar, who had been sitting and drinking on the stoop with his friend Mr. Jay, had fallen over backward onto the stone steps leading to the base-ment and fractured his skull.

Oscar spent almost five weeks in the municipal hospital where he was rushed by ambulance after his fall. During the first week Gloria took the long bus trip to the hospital each day and stood in the crowded ward beside the bed where her husband was at-tached to many machines that seemed to be doing everything for him. During this entire week Oscar remained unconscious. On the few occasions when Gloria was able to find a doctor to talk with, he had never been very encouraging. For the first few days there was some question about whether Oscar would live at all. Then the doctors began to talk about extensive damage and possi-ble paralysis.

In addition to visiting Oscar in the hospital, Gloria had to deal with the financial side of this tragedy. Oscar's present hospitaliza-tion would be covered by his employer-sponsored medical in-surance, at least at the beginning. The doctor's descriptions of the injury seemed to indicate that Oscar would have to stay in the hospital well beyond the coverage period. In addition, because

the accident had not occurred on the job, Oscar was not eligible
for workmen's compensation, and his paychecks would stop after
his first week in the hospital. Some of Oscar's co-workers contributed to a small fund for his family, but this amount couldn't
make up even for one paycheck. Gloria talked with the company
manager, who agreed to give Oscar pay for his vacation at this
time but said he could do nothing more. The social worker at the
hospital suggested to Gloria that she apply to welfare. Gloria did
this.

Because the welfare office is located several miles in the opposite direction from the hospital and because it took an entire
day just to make an appointment for an interview, Gloria was
unable to visit Oscar for several days. She was anxious about this
and tried to do some of the work with the welfare department by
telephone. The department refused to talk about the problem or
to set up an appointment by telephone. Instead they told Gloria
to gather together all the information available about Oscar's job,
including several months of pay stubs; records of his insurance
coverage; information about the family, including birth records;
information about household expenses, including rent receipts
and utility bills; and any papers relating to his current hospi-
talized state. Gloria was told to bring these papers with her to the
district welfare office.

Gloria was glad she had followed Dee Dee's advice and gone to
the welfare office at 7:30 A.M. This meant she was close to the
front of the line that had already begun to form outside the locked
and guarded building. When the guards unlocked the doors at 9
A.M. there was a rush of bodies toward the intake desk, where
people were assigned numbers and told to wait again. Many of
those who arrived at 9 A.M. as directed did not receive a number
and were locked out when the guards closed the doors because the
intake workers claimed to have given out more appointments
than could possibly be processed that day. Gloria had received a
number and spent only three hours waiting on the hard wooden
chairs crowded together in the center of the large, barnlike, first-
floor hall of the center. Many people were not able to sit down. A
number of people were called and sent upstairs, where they also
waited.

Those who went upstairs were able to see both Black and

White welfare workers as they chatted, visited each other's desks, drank coffee, ate doughnuts, sold Avon and other products to each other, read the morning paper, or otherwise avoided seeing clients long past the 9 A.M. beginning of the working day. All this went on in full view of the welfare applicants and clients, who were assigned to seats along the wall. Mothers with tiny infants and small children, addicts, old men and women, and people of many colors and ethnic descriptions sat and waited.

Gloria's number was called and she was asked to fill out an application form. The worker said the applications could not be processed or otherwise acted upon the same day they were taken in. Now Gloria would receive a unit number. She was to return in three days, again bringing all the information and records with her.

While waiting for this brief conference, Gloria saw a number of people she recognized, including two women from the block. It was one of these women who pointed out to her the speed with which one of the less docile male clients seemed to move in the system. The woman claimed that she had been present last week when that same client, whom she described as an addict, grew tired of being put off and ordered around and threatened the welfare worker, first verbally and finally with a knife. Such tactics didn't always work, since the district office was manned by uniformed guards with guns and truncheons. But when they did succeed, most of the onlookers, who would never do the same thing themselves, did not seem upset or disapproving. As the woman was saying to Gloria, anything that got done as the result of such a threat could as easily have been done without it if the welfare workers and the system wanted it to be done.

Gloria felt tired and frustrated about the entire interaction with the welfare people. This was her first experience with it. Although she had heard stories by others, the firsthand experience was a shock. Gloria didn't look forward to repeating this process three days in the future. But if she had to do so, she would. With Oscar in the hospital someone had to provide for the Ward family. Today's trip merely meant that she had a unit number to present to the intake desk next time. And now Gloria felt too tired to make the trip to the hospital in time for evening visiting hours.

With Oscar still unconscious it all seemed so meaningless anyway. And the washing and ironing were piling up. She decided to have one of the boys go to the hospital.

It was from Gloria, other family members, and friends that Oscar was to hear about his hospital stay. He had only flashes of remembrance of those weeks. Oscar didn't remember anything until he was well enough to sit up in a wheelchair in the hall with the other patients who were able to be out of bed. Some of the others were even tied up into a sitting position. They moved anyone into the hallway as soon as possible because the bed space was needed for more serious cases, or at least that was what the nurse told Gloria.

Oscar did remember being embarrassed by the urine bag that hung on the side of his wheelchair, to be seen by anyone who got off the elevator on that floor. When his youngest daughter's godparents came to visit, Oscar asked Val to talk to someone about moving him out of this public area. The best that could be done, according to the staff, was to turn the chair so that the bag didn't show, and although the nurse promised to keep this in mind in the future, it was not done. Through it all Oscar felt powerless and helpless. He remained in this section of the hospital just over four weeks.

When he returned home it was with a cane, appointments for physiotherapy sessions, and the ominous news that he would never be able to work at his present job again. This decision was agreed on by both the hospital doctors and the doctor representing the firm. Oscar felt totally useless.

During the latter part of Oscar's hospital stay, Gloria had made several more trips back to the welfare department office. She had finally been able to register the Ward family as welfare clients. The payment each week was to be much less than Oscar's paycheck, and she had just barely been able to manage with that. And this was the first time the entire family had ever received welfare. Gloria didn't feel good about it. In addition she had not yet received a check, but the department promised that one would be forthcoming within the next two weeks. In the meantime Gloria borrowed money from Bea and others for immediate expenses. The welfare department urged Gloria to look into the possibility that Oscar would be eligible for social security disability payments from the federal government, thus freeing the state totally from any support payments.

For Oscar, the thought of not working after a solid twenty-four years as a working man with one company was inconceivable. At first he refused to believe it. He even made the trip by bus up to the plant where he had worked all these years. His former fellow workers and the office manager were pleasant, but nothing could be done to get his job back. Oscar didn't even keep up with the physiotherapy sessions. He felt that if the doctors were sure and final in their decision that he would never be able to work again, he didn't care whether he had trouble keeping his balance at times or if his left hand and arm were less useful than before the fall. He had little use for them. Without a job, without being able to support his family, Oscar saw himself as worthless.

In the Ghetto: The Wilsons

EVEN IN BARE FEET, Hank's 6′3″ height made him stand out, and in his fashionable high-heeled platform boots he had been an exceptional figure among the crowd that had stood watching a fire rage through the local dry-cleaning shop. Perhaps because he stood so tall, he had been able to see the firemen break open the fire-blackened cash register and pocket the paper money before throwing the loose change onto the ground. As the coins had hit the pavement, many people, most of them children or young people, had begun to scoop up the rolling coins. And the uniformed policemen, standing by while the register was axed open by the firemen, had swung their clubs and chased people away from the scattered coins.

Hank had never thought of himself as a militant. But he saw this as some horrible game in which the Black people were offered small change and kept from getting even that. Hank had moved to Blackston from the South. He had lived here long enough not to have much respect for these uniformed people who came into the community from the outside. But this was a new experience to add to his view of them.

Today, while his own house was burning down, Hank thought

back on that scene in front of the cleaners. Perhaps that was what made him push his way back into his two-story brick house, which now stood burned, wrecked, and drenched. He pushed right past the fireman and policeman who stood talking together at the front door. They had already talked with Hank and knew that he was the owner of the house. Hank arrived in his front bedroom just in time to see a fireman going through the dresser drawers and putting items into the pockets of his voluminous black rubber coat. When Hank and the firefighter reached into the back of the next drawer and both found at the same time the sock in which Hank had hidden his folding money, the fireman said that he had been looking for items that would be returned to the owner. Hank took the money. But since the fireman did not then or later offer to return any of the items from his coat pockets, Hank didn't believe the explanation.

Instead he left the house and began to try to organize a few people to help him rescue any salvageable items. Some of the furniture, particularly the bedroom set, on which he still had many payments to make, might be saved. The items toward the back of the house, including a large, new refrigerator freezer and an avocado-colored gas range, recently bought to match the kitchen floor tiles, were totally destroyed, along with everything in the two back bedrooms.

Hank looked at what was left of the floor tiles and paneling he had installed throughout the house and realized that it was a total loss. This struck Hank especially hard for two reasons. First, he knew that the fire insurance he was forced to pay through the bank mortgage payments covered only the house, not personal items such as furniture or improvements such as paneling and tile. In addition, Hank knew that the tiles and paneling represented a large part of his income in that they had been made available in place of wages.

Hank worked at installing paneling and tiles for others. He liked his work, though it was sporadic and unpredictable in terms of both what he would be paid for a given job and how much time he would have to spend at it. In addition, usually he had steady work in the spring and summer but not at other times. Hank's boss for some time had been a Jewish entrepreneur who arranged with real estate agents to repair and remodel houses or apartments or to build finished basements. Often in order to win a bid he made unreasonable promises to finish the job within a certain time period. This meant that Hank worked twelve to eighteen hours a day. Hank didn't mind doing this occasionally, since it usually meant he would receive extra pay. But this wasn't always the case, and sometimes the boss wouldn't even come around at the end of the week at all, so that the workers didn't get paid until the following week unless they took the time off to chase the boss down. The boss often didn't answer his home phone, and he was rarely at his office, since he spent a good deal of time with potential clients or wholesalers or other business friends. Besides, if Hank and his fellow workers went off hunting the boss, they couldn't finish the job by the deadline and wouldn't get paid as much as promised.

Hank enjoyed the work. Especially when it wasn't a rush job, he enjoyed the freedom he had to start and stop when he chose, so long as the work was finished when promised. He liked working with his friends. He enjoyed being able to buy a pint of liquor and have a drink while he worked. The job required that the workers be jacks of many trades in addition to laying tile and installing paneling. Hank's best fellow worker, Smiley, was very good at plumbing work, and Calvin was a fair electrician. Sometimes, especially if the job had to pass inspection, Calvin would do the actual work while the boss brought a licensed electrician to the job to meet with the inspector. Hank himself knew of a good many Black and Spanish men who did similar work at lower wages than those with licenses or formal training. But he preferred to work with Smiley and Calvin. Sometimes his brother Jack went with him too. They were all good friends and worked well together. Neither Smiley nor Calvin lived in Blackston now, but they often met at Hank's house and partied together or helped each other work on their own houses, or did odd jobs for neighbors from each area.

The fact that they were able to improve their own houses was one of the side benefits of this kind of job. In fact, they were convinced that the boss knew it was a benefit and used it as an excuse to pay them low wages. They were able to improve their own houses by buying supplies such as tile and wall paneling in the boss's name at dealers where he had arranged a discount because of the large amount of business he did. Hank was constantly aware that at any time his employer might feel that Hank had overstepped some unspecified limit and that this might serve as grounds for firing him. The boss also paid lower wages in the belief that the worker would make it up through theft. The worker had less money wages, all the uncertainty of the situation, and was, in addition, at a moral disadvantage. Hank was very careful not to buy excess supplies too often. Sometimes he used them for his own home improvement, and sometimes he resold them at full cost with or without labor for the improvement of his neighbors' homes.

Buying at wholesale in the boss's name had enabled Hank to fix up the second floor of the house he had recently set about buying. He asked for and got a security deposit from the anthropologists who wanted to move from the tenement across the street and was able to use this money to buy some of the materials at cut rate. But money wasn't always available, and buying supplies cheaply wasn't much of a benefit unless you had money to invest in such things. So most of the time the benefit of supplies at cost wasn't much of a benefit at all, and Hank would have preferred cash wages in hand.

This was the position that Smiley's wife took too, to hear him tell it. She wanted him to save up money and get them out of the ghetto rather than fix up the rickety frame house in which they'd been living for so long. It was toward this end that she had gone to work too. But most of the money seemed to go into things to keep the household running. They still didn't get out of the ghetto.

Hank stood looking at the fire-ruined walls and floor. He remembered that in his own case it had been possible to buy the materials because he had finished and been paid for one large job. He and Bernice had discussed it and agreed to invest the money from that job in fixing up the house and to try to get along on her welfare payment to meet their food and mortgage needs. Bernice had a teenage son for whom she had been receiving some supplemental payments. When Hank and Bernice had decided to get married, she had not informed the welfare department and still continued to receive payment for her teenage son. Hank lost his job shortly thereafter, and the welfare payments were their only steady income. It had been a lean time. Now here it was all burned up and he wasn't one step ahead.

Thank goodness Bernice and his baby Tylee were safe. Tylee wasn't Bernice's first child but he was Hank's first and so far only child, so he felt very strongly about him. He hadn't even been very happy when Bernice proposed paying for Tylee's birth on her welfare medical coverage. She could do this if Tylee was described as illegitimate and received his mother's maiden name at birth. But now Hank had to admit that even the slight increase in welfare payment to cover Tylee had been irreplaceable. Hank worked hard and well, but it was Bernice who had the business sense in the family.

Well, the way to take care of them now was to rescue as much as possible from this house and to decide with Bernice what to do next. Bernice was down the street with Hank's sister Velma and her three small girls. Velma's common-law husband, Steve, the father of her third daughter, had arrived back on the block at the same time as the fire engines. Hank remembered noticing that it was Steve who had supplied a coat and slippers to Val, who had come down the burning stairs naked with his son Jonathan in his arms.

Hank saw a number of people standing around and asked his brother Jack to help move things into Velma's basement. Jack's friend Randy was there too, so Hank promised them both some cash to help move things. Hank was well aware that both Randy and Jack were heroin addicts, but this wasn't a consideration to bother him. He knew from long experience with his brother and his brother's friends that this was a situation in which neither Jack nor Randy would steal from him. In fact he trusted them more than he trusted the police or firemen who had just gone.

Hank arranged the moving and went to join Val and Betty-lou, who were talking with a man Hank had met earlier. This man was an inspector with the fire department and would be writing up the report on the fire. Hank stood quietly while Val, wearing only a raincoat and slippers to protect him from the March cold, pointed out that it was the fire department that had caused this blaze. Hank nodded in agreement as Val described the fire that had taken place in the house next door just before midnight last night. He pointed out that the firemen who had come at that time, in addition to breaking out all the windows in the house and soaking it with water, had thrown the mattress in which the fire had started into the airshaft between the two houses. Presumably the mattress smoldered during the intervening six hours and burst into flame about 6 A.M., starting the fire that had just destroyed Hank's house.

The fire inspector suggested that this was only a guess about what happened. He refused to go into either house to look at the mattress, which was still in the airshaft. He did not deny that a mattress was indeed there or that there had been a fire in the house next door just a few hours earlier. He even knew from the report at the firehouse that it had been started by an electric heater placed too close to the bed. But he pointed out that no one had actually seen the start of the second fire. He rejected Hank's comment that the fire was first seen in and did most damage to their living room, whose windows opened onto the airshaft. The fire inspector refused to list any of this information in his report. He merely walked away, saying that a copy of his report would be available through the municipal government in a week or two.

Hank asked about Jonathan and was directed to look across the street to Aunt Bea's window, where both Jonathan and Aunt Bea were watching the activities. Hank suggested that they all get back to work picking out the things to be saved. The insurance company, which Bernice had contacted from Velma's house, had already sent around a panel truck with plywood boards and two workers to begin nailing up the gaping windows that no longer had glass or bars to protect them. Since the gas and electricity had been shut off, the house was rapidly becoming pitch black as each window was covered with wood. Hank was able to get the men to hold off a little while from putting boards over the large kitchen windows that supplied the only daylight upstairs and down. The men went onto the roof to nail over the skylight opening. Mr. Gardner from next door brought over a long-handled flashlight and a large battery light. Hank took the latter and went into the basement to look for his own tool chest, where he had a flashlight and some needed tools.

Jack, Randy, Jim B., Val, Bettylou, and her friend Wilma were carrying out large pieces of furniture and large plastic sacks full of small items. Hank knew that the Valentines' things were going into the basement of friends two doors away. But this took some careful packing, since the basement of their house was flooded by runoff from the two fires. Hank found his tools and flashlight and went up the stairs to the second floor of his house. He wanted to see how much damage had been done to the tenant's apartment. Hank watched while Val put on a pair of shoes that had survived the fire inside the portable wardrobe they had bought for the closetless second floor. Hank's own clothes had been destroyed. They had hung in the only built-in closet in the entire house. That closet was in the Wilsons' kitchen, which had been totally burned out. Val pointed out to Hank that although most of his clothes had survived the fire, almost a thousand books had been burned or otherwise destroyed by axe-wielding firemen. Hank was a newspaper reader and didn't care much for books, and Val wasn't very clothing-oriented. So although the two could sympathize about each other's losses, their specific interests were quite different. Hank expressed to Val his despair about the money and work represented by the once-paneled walls that now stood bare from the beams to the debris-covered floors.

But Hank was young and practical. He was just twenty-five years old and buying a house. So he went back downstairs and back to work on his own house. He would have to contact Smiley to tell him that he wouldn't come to the job that day and possibly not for a few days. There was so much to do here. But if he didn't get back to the job with Smiley and Calvin, he wouldn't have any money this week either. There didn't seem to be any way to win. There was no such thing as sick leave or vacation time from this job. If you didn't work, you didn't get paid.

BERNICE SAT AT HER sister-in-law's kitchen table and thought about some of the same problems. Tylee and Velma's three girls had been sent to the living room and told to play quietly, but Bernice's thoughts were still interrupted by her Uncle Jonesy, who came in and out with running reports on the cleanup. Bernice's German shepherd and the Valentines' dog were both temporarily here at Velma's and trying to work out living space. Steve, Velma's common-law husband, was asking for breakfast before he went off to his job as a shoe salesman far across town in a new shopping center. And occasionally Jack or Randy was sent by Hank to get some instructions from Bernice or to bring some less burned item into Velma's house rather than into the basement. Bernice was also on the telephone trying to reach the bank, the welfare department, and the insurance agent, who had promised to come when she called over two hours ago.

Bernice, who was six years older than her husband, Hank, did not look it. In contrast to him she was not tall and was slight of build. Bernice had a well-proportioned face that could look quite different depending on hair style, wig, or head wrap. Today she merely looked harried, since her hair was unset and she was still wearing the bathrobe she had thrown on when she first saw the flames, woke Hank, and ran upstairs to warn the tenants.

Occasionally Bernice thought about the six-year age difference between Hank and herself. She had thought about it more when she and Hank first started going together. At that time he had only been up from the South, where he was born and raised, for a short time. He was extremely thin then, and this made him look even younger than his years. He came to Blackston and to Paul Street because of family connections. Hank's oldest sister, Tommy, had been married to Bernice's father's brother, Uncle Jonesy. The two had remained formally married but had separated years ago, with Tommy returning to the South and Uncle Jonesy moving to Paul Street after giving up his career as a merchant seaman. When Velma came North she had moved to Blackston even though she had two brothers in other parts of the metropolitan area. Before Hank decided to come North he had seen pictures of Bernice, Uncle Jonesy's niece, and had been attracted to her even then. As far as Bernice was aware, most of the people she knew in Blackston did not regard an adult's age as very important when forming social or sexual ties. So Hank and Bernice became friends, intimates, and finally husband and wife.

One effect of the age difference was that Bernice had lived a longer and more varied life before she met Hank. In addition, most of Bernice's experiences had taken place in large northern cities, while Hank had lived in a semirural town that existed solely as a depot for the surrounding tobacco farms. Often the two compared their experiences and knowledge of people and generally agreed that, as far as they could see, people were much the same everywhere. These family discussions often included Uncle Jonesy, whose family had come from New Orleans before his brother, Bernice's father, had moved to the northern city where she was born. Steve, Velma's man, was from a different state in the South. He too would join the discussions with relish, bragging about his home state, Georgia, its nice people, and its famous Geechee cooking.

Bernice could already foresee the mixture of cooking styles that would be required for the next few weeks. It seemed clear to her that she, Hank, and Tylee would have to stay with Velma and Steve, Uncle Jonesy, Jack, and the four girls.

Bernice had seen the welfare hotel where the Red Cross or the social-service department would probably put them if they appealed for emergency lodging. The place had recently been written up in the morning paper. The newspaper stories, illustrated with pictures of the horrible conditions, started after a young child had fallen to his death in an unused and unprotected elevator shaft. The social-service department paid scandalous rates to house large families in small rooms in a building that was dirty, had no restaurant or cooking facilities, no working elevators, and poor services in other respects. The hotel owners were making more money housing welfare clients with no place to go than they had made when the building was operated as a regular hotel offering restaurants, daily maid service, and working elevators. Bernice refused to go to a welfare hotel. She knew that the family next door, whose house had burned around midnight, had gone to such a place. They were recent arrivals on Paul Street and had no friends or relatives who could put them up.

Velma, who was even more casual and expansive than her brother Hank, had already assumed that they would all stay with her. Unfortunately, Velma's casualness extended to her housekeeping too, which didn't please Bernice much. Bernice planned to get Velma's two older girls, Georgette and Marisa, to work at cleaning up the house as soon as things settled down. They were used to working for Auntie Bernice and were even now taking care of Tylee and their younger sister, Nanette. Velma hadn't sent them to school today because they had been awakened by the 6 A.M. fire.

Bernice and Velma talked about how they would combine their

welfare checks, buy food stamps, and shop together for both families, including Uncle Jonesy and Jack, whose home in Hank's basement was also gone. Perhaps something could be fixed up in the basement here, or the two men could sleep during the day, as they often did. Perhaps Jack would go back to "catting" around the neighborhood, sleeping wherever and in whatever position he ended up when his friends couldn't go on drinking, talking, or whatever any longer. There were a number of men around Paul Street who catted. Jack and Randy's friend Jim B. had a brother-in-law who had spent time with several Paul Street residents. He had been thrown out of his sister's home after a family argument, and Aunt Bea had taken him in for a few months. Most catting was done a day at a time, though, involved no commitment or responsibility, and was probably most prevalent among families that had young sons or friends.

Bernice and Velma had been friends for a long time. Bernice reminded Velma about the time they each had an apartment in the tenement across the street where Aunt Bea and the Wards now lived. Only a six-foot hallway separated their two front doors, and often it was difficult to know exactly who lived where, since they spent so much time in each other's apartments. Bernice liked to think about it, since this was also the period when Hank had begun courting her. Hank had moved into Bernice's apartment after they were married.

Velma pointed out that they had almost lived together when Hank had brought their mother up to Blackston to have a serious operation. Hank did not feel that the semisegregated southern hospital available to his mother was good enough. So he took off from his work, drove South, picked up his mother, and brought her back to Blackston. She entered the nearby Jewish hospital. The doctors had found it necessary to amputate her right leg above the knee. During her convalescence, Mother Wilson lived with Velma. Velma had already moved across the street into a two-family brick house. It was rumored that the house belonged to Uncle Jonesy, purchased through his merchant-seaman earnings. By this time Uncle Jonesy and Tommy had been separated for some years. Uncle Jonesy seemed to have almost no expenses. He rarely wore any clothes other than a workshirt, pants, and an old paint cap. He ate occasionally with relatives and slept in the

basement of the house. He seemed to have no fixed respon-
sibilities. Maybe the rumors were true. People in Blackston didn't
pry into each other's money matters.

Bernice, Velma, Hank, Jack, and Uncle Jonesy helped to care
for Mother Wilson. Although they were spread out over three
separate households, they functioned together for the two months
Mother Wilson lived with Velma and learned to use her new
metal leg device. When she came up for the operation, Mother
Wilson had left her own second family in the South. Her son Bob
and his wife had been killed in an automobile accident in this
same metropolitan area. Their surviving daughter and two young
sons went South to live with Mother Wilson. On the whole,
Mother Wilson hadn't found them too much of a burden. Her
own youngest child, Hank, had only recently left home, and it
was good to have some young people around again. This had been
a number of years ago; her granddaughter was just finishing high
school and the two boys were still in grammar school when
Mother Wilson went for her operation. Tommy, who then lived
some distance away on the coast, drove over to Mother Wilson's
during her absence to check up on the three young people. She
had the impression that the girl was too serious about her
boyfriend, but Tommy didn't feel it was her place to interfere.

Velma and Bernice heard this from Tommy only after Mother
Wilson had telephoned to ask Velma a favor some four months
after she returned South from her hospital stay. Her granddaughter had graduated from high school and had tried unsuc-
cessfully to find a job in the small town. Now she was pregnant
and didn't want to marry the boy. Mother Wilson asked whether
the girl could come North and stay with Velma until she had the
baby. Hank and Bernice had just bought the house up the street
and were very busy cleaning it out and repairing it. Besides,
Mother Wilson had heard that Bernice's own teenage son had just
been sent to stay with Bernice's mother. It seemed clear that the
couple might not want a teenager around while they were still
working out their own young marriage.

The entire family enjoyed having Bob's daughter around. She
was cheerful and helpful though very confused about what she
wanted to do. After the baby was born, she gave him to Velma to
bring up and returned to Mother Wilson's alone. But Velma had

kept the baby for only three months when the teenage mother decided that she wanted to care for her own son after all; Mother Wilson had agreed that she could cope with a great-grandson in the house.

So the Wilsons' extended family expanded, contracted, moved into separate houses, traveled north and south, depending on the circumstances and needs of each individual. And the present fire was a situation where they would have to come together again.

Velma and Bernice began to review their present cash and food supplies and to anticipate the next welfare check. This would be Bernice and Hank's only source of money until he was able to return to work. Bernice planned to call her welfare worker and appeal to him for some supplemental money because of the fire losses.

The woman who had lived in this house before Velma had been active in the Welfare Rights Organization. Although Velma and Bernice often talked with her about welfare rules and activities, they did not want to become members of the Welfare Rights group. They had seen pictures of welfare recipients blocking doors or sitting in at the welfare office. Bernice and Velma did not want their pictures in the paper. They felt that their welfare status was a private matter between themselves and the postman. Bernice expressed it in terms of keeping up friendly relations with the welfare caseworker in the hope that the worker would in turn be helpful to them. Welfare regulations changed rapidly, and many of them were unknown to the clients. It was Bernice's belief, based on experience, that the rules were flexible enough so that a caseworker could get benefits for a client which the client did not even know were available, or could interpret the rules so as to help or hinder a client.

Hank did not particularly approve of this approach. He had a grudging admiration for the Welfare Rights group. When they had talked about it over the newspaper stories and pictures, it had become clear that they differed on the subject, but where welfare payments were concerned Bernice had the final word. It was her maiden name that appeared first on the mailbox, and when the welfare worker on one of his rare visits had seen the name Wilson on the mailbox too, Bernice explained that the landlord used this address to receive his mail. So the welfare department continued to pay Bernice's rent allowance to Mr. Wilson, the landlord, never knowing that he was also Mr. Wilson, Bernice's husband.

Bernice had argued for this arrangement. She liked to have nice clothes, nice furniture, and a little money to spend. She also wanted to get off of Paul Street and out of Blackston. Even though she had been receiving welfare payments for some time now, she never seemed to get ahead. Bernice started to scratch some figures onto the back of an envelope with a pencil stub she found on top of the refrigerator. Here she received a welfare supplement of about $100 a month for herself, her teenage son, and the baby, Tylee. In addition, her rent was paid by the welfare department to Hank Wilson, and the upstairs tenants paid $150 a month in rent. Hank worked as often as possible. Yet by the time they paid the monthly mortgage payment, the insurance payment, and the payments on the bedroom suite and the refrigerator-freezer and range, bought food, paid for light and gas and oil, got clothes from the dry cleaners, repaid debts, and kept Hank's truck running, there was hardly enough for entertainment or new clothes.

Bernice liked clothes and would tell anybody so. It was for this reason, combined with the lack of money to buy all the clothes she wanted, that Bernice sewed a lot. She was very competent and interested in the latest fashions. Because she was an accomplished seamstress, both she and Hank dressed better than their income would otherwise allow. This was an important saving in such a clothes-conscious community. It was Bernice's observation that she, like the people around her, had dressed up most often as a teenager and young adult. Now, as a young married person, her dress-up periods alternated with long spells in a housecoat or bathrobe. She hoped she would never reach the stage of some of the older people in the community, who seemed to wear fine clothes only on special occasions two or three times a year.

Despite all this work and hustling, all they had to show for it was a burned-out house and some burned-up clothes and a battered panel truck that Bernice couldn't even drive. Most of the time Hank took it on jobs and used it to pick up supplies or to dump materials from the apartments and basements he renovated. It was useful to take across town to the discount food market where she and Velma liked to shop. When there was any cash available, Bernice got Hank to take them shopping on the weekend between welfare checks, since the stores were so much less crowded then and store prices were not raised in anticipation of welfare shoppers. But Velma didn't usually have money then, and they would be unable to buy the food coupons that provided a small additional saving. Hank occasionally took Bernice to visit friends outside of Blackston in the truck. But all in all it seemed little enough for the work and effort she and Hank put into living.

Bernice finally reached her welfare worker at the local office. He promised to call the fire department to verify the facts of the emergency and to try to find some additional help for Bernice. Bernice explained that she was going to move in temporarily with a friend on the same street until she was able to find other housing. She hinted that she would like to move back into her old apartment if Mr. Wilson the landlord could repair it quickly enough. Bernice was taking a chance that the amount allowed her by the welfare to replace her furniture would be greater than the amount she would lose when they deducted for the unpaid rent. She also intended to appeal to the caseworker for some payment to Velma and Steve, since they could not be expected to put her up indefinitely for free. But all that was in the future. Bernice was sure that the worker would come around to verify her account of events, and she could appeal to him in person then.

Bernice hung up the phone and went back to talking to Velma about the fire between trips to the front porch and hallway to bring into the apartment items that Jack and Randy were still moving over from the house. Bernice pointed out that she was much less trusting of Randy than Hank was. As a person who had been around and thought of herself as worldly wise, Bernice would have hated herself if she thought she had allowed an addict to rip her off through casualness or excess kindness on her part.

She hadn't been at all pleased with herself or Hank when his brother Jack had taken their expensive stereo and hi-fi equipment almost two years ago. They had not seen him take it, but no one else could have done so without breaking in. And Jack, who had been living in their house before the theft, then disappeared for months. Her anger was even greater than Hank's. Hank's anger was combined with personal hurt, because he considered it not only theft but a rejection or breaking of family ties and obligations on Jack's part. Up to that time Jack, who had been on and off heroin for at least twenty years, had not been using much lately. He had most often been straight enough to go with Hank on jobs for a number of weeks off and on. During this time he had also helped with the cooking and cleaning. Jack had been staying in the basement, sleeping on an old couch. He had protected the house both by his own physical presence and because the basement served as a place where his friends could meet. Addicts did not generally steal where they and fellow addicts lived. Sometimes this unspoken rule was broken, but when it was even the addict culprit never admitted to stealing from friends.

It had been months before Jack had come around again. And he totally denied the theft. Hank's anger had ebbed. He had got rid of much of it by cursing Jack to their mutual friends. Finally both Hank and Bernice, like their neighbors all over Blackston, came to accept what seemed inevitable. Theft was common, and eventually Bernice and Hank came to blame themselves for their trust and casualness more than they blamed the thief. So for many months following the theft they had been much more careful. They didn't let anyone use the basement; they didn't socialize with anyone they identified as an addict; they wouldn't let Jim B. or Randy into the house; and they never left the house unwatched by some person. Even their German shepherd, who was supposed to be a watchdog, had too many friends among potential thieves. Eventually this wariness decreased. One important reason for the change was that it kept Bernice and Hank from enjoying the sociability that is an important emotional outlet and support in a community like Blackston. Now even after such a traumatic event Jack was living with the family again and playing a useful social role.

Hank and Jack came to announce that most of the items worth saving from the house had been moved. Hank asked Jack to watch things while the tenants continued to clean out the upstairs; he said he was going to find Smiley and try to make some arrangement about his job. Bernice agreed to stay at Velma's and to meet with the representative from the insurance company if he arrived while Hank was gone. Randy went off to help the Valentines, and

Bernice chased away the large group of preteenagers who had been trooping from one house to the other looking for something to do. Steve had gone off to work and wouldn't be back for hours since the shoe store was open late on Friday nights. Tylee and Nanette were asleep, and the two older girls were watching TV.

Bernice and Velma sat down and began to eat a little from the pot of grits and the still-warm sausages that had been breakfast for Steve and the girls. Bernice began talking about the clothes that had burned up and recalled that among them were the things she had made for the fashion show last weekend. The fashion show had been an event organized by the social club that Bernice and Hank had joined, and was sponsored by their next-door neighbors, the Gardners, who had recently moved onto Paul Street.

Velma knew that the Gardners were only a little older than Bernice, and she felt that they served as a model for Bernice. The Gardners were both employed, they owned two cars, and the Paul Street house into which they had moved was the second house they were in the process of buying. Bernice, who lived directly next door, knew from watching the mailman that Miz Gardner was receiving a welfare check too. Miz Gardner worked during the day, and Mr. Gardner had a night-shift job. Their children ranged from young adults to teenagers and preteens. Mr. Gardner left the oldest girl, who had a daughter of her own, to care for the younger ones while he provided janitor service in his two houses. It was not at all unusual to see Mr. Gardner out sweeping the porch steps and sidewalk, painting the trim, or repairing the fence in the backyard. On several occasions he even took a pail and mop and mopped the porch, steps, and sidewalk area in front of his house.

The social club, as Bernice had explained to Velma before, was another idea of Mr. Gardner's that was meant to provide sociability and contacts while making a profit. When he explained it to Bernice, he pointed out that there was both a women's and a men's club, both called the Cameos. Each person invited to join the club put up a certain amount of money. This seed money was used to set up a social event such as a cocktail sip, card party, fashion show, or formal dance. Admission tickets would be printed up and sold in any ghetto areas where members had connections and at their jobs. The tickets would cost less if purchased before the event rather than at the door on the night of the event. In addition to admission, each guest would pay for food and drinks. At the end of each event the proceeds would be divided equally among the members who had worked on that event. At the end of the year any money left in the club treasury would be split among the members. Each member was expected to host at least one event, and all members were expected to work on each social occasion. It had sounded like a great way to make money, and Bernice talked Hank into joining. Hank was a little hesitant about the membership fee, which had to be paid in a lump sum, but Bernice convinced him it would be worth it. For Mr. Gardner it was certainly worth it, since it provided new contacts to whom he could sell the shipments of "hot" clothing he received rather regularly.

Last week's fashion show had been held in the Gardners' basement, where they had set up a small kitchen area, a bar, and a jukebox. On most weekend nights Mr. Gardner ran card games and sold fried fish, fried chicken, and french fries in the basement. He had agreed to rent it to Bernice, whose own basement had not yet been finished, although Hank had been promising to work on it for weeks.

Bernice's fashion show was a big social occasion among various age groups on Paul Street. The younger people were interested in their age mate, a young transvestite, who was to model satin hot pants, and an exotic dancer who was not from Blackston. Some other young people and a number of slightly older women were going to be in the show, along with a number of small children, including Bernice's and Velma's daughters, Jonathan Valentine, and Mr. Gardner's grandchild. Everyone was making or buying or otherwise fixing up clothes to wear in the fashion show or at the dance to follow.

Bernice and Velma recalled their own hectic preparations. Velma had made matching velvet vests and pants for her two girls. Bernice had made a green knicker suit and blouse for Tylee, a brocade and velvet suit for Hank, and a floor-length dress for herself. All these things had been burned up in the morning's fire. Besides the sewing, both Bernice and Velma had been involved in selling tickets, decorating, buying the food and liquor, arrangements for cooking, and as a special favor the training of Clarence.

Clarence, or Clara, as he preferred to be called, was an eighteen-year-old male who wanted desperately to be a female. After graduating from high school he had worked in a department store downtown but had quit because of an argument with the section manager. Although Clara's sexual interests and aspirations were well known to anyone on the block or in the general area who cared to look or listen, Clara had never before had a chance to make an official appearance as a female. He wanted to do so at the fashion show and appealed to Bernice and Velma to help prepare for the event.

Bernice, Velma, Bettylou, and whoever else happened to be around had sat at this very table for several evenings while Bernice taught Clara how to apply makeup, and both Bernice and Velma had by example as well as words tried to teach Clara to walk in a way that was considered feminine by the gathered company. In turn Clara regaled the group with stories about his friends and their reactions to his coming out. One night Jack and Hank had come in while the lessons were going on. They had joined in too. Jack had even made mock passes at Clara, which seemed to please him and amuse everyone else.

Velma's direct question to her sister-in-law about the profits made from the fashion show brought the reminiscing to a halt. Bernice had hoped to make more money than she and Hank finally received after everything had been paid for and the money divided among people whom Bernice felt hadn't worked as hard as she had.

But Bernice was still hopeful that the Cameo Club would serve as a source of income that could go toward improving their situation. Bernice had done office work before Tylee was born, and she was considering it again now. Somehow the money earned at the kind of work Bernice could find went mostly toward transportation, lunches, and the clothes required by such a job. Bernice also took into account what was lost in terms of child care, homemade clothes, and home-cooked meals. For although Velma would care for Tylee, she couldn't always be asked to do it for free while Bernice earned money. And Bernice wasn't sure she wanted the obligation that would develop. Also, Bernice had her own views on child rearing as well as housekeeping, and they didn't always agree with Velma's. The time demands of a job and travel would make it less likely that she would want to come home and sew. But she would need more clothes, and there would be such a temptation to buy them in the stores that were sure to be around an office location. Bernice realized that her cooking expenses would go up too, since she wouldn't be home to cook the slow and cheap dishes that were among Hank's favorites. Instead of hamhocks and pinto beans she would probably buy more expensive but fast-cooking meats or prepared foods. Either way Hank wouldn't like it.

Bernice had a final consideration that she had voiced to her tenant and friend Bettylou not so long ago. Bernice felt that if she worked and had a steady income, however small, Hank would be less motivated to work each day. Hank was a good worker but he enjoyed friends, leisure, and being with his family more. Most important, his desire to improve their status and to get out of Blackston was not as great as Bernice's.

IT WAS HARD FOR Hank to believe that three years had gone by since the big fire in his house. He remembered saying then that the place was cursed and he didn't want to live there any more. But he had lived there two years more after repairing it. As of this month it was a year since he and his family had moved into an all-Black community of one- and two-family houses a dozen miles fom Blackston. He had never really expected that he would be off of Paul Street and out of Blackston. And he really wasn't. Even Hank was amused that he and Bernice and Jack spent almost as much time on Paul Street now that they no longer lived there as they had before. Today as Hank sat on the wooden bench on the porch of his old house talking with people as they came by, he was aware of how much had happened in those three years. In some ways it still seemed like old times. Bernice was across the street drinking vodka and grapefruit juice with Aunt Bea and her new husband. Jack was down near the corner store sitting in a car and drinking with some other dudes. Hank had been invited to join them, but he preferred to sit here in the open, listening to the music that was coming out of the window behind him, and thinking about things.

Sitting here in front of a house that he was still buying and whose mortgage was covered by the high welfare rent he received for the two large families who lived there made Hank think back to when times had seemed less bright. After the fire, when the insurance money had come through, Hank had arranged to have his boss bid on repairing the house. That way Hank could work on his own house and be paid for it. And if he decided to cut any corners, the difference between what the insurance paid and what he and Bernice were willing to settle for became profit for them. He even finished the job rather rapidly, since the joint living arrangement that put six adults and four children into Velma's five rooms had begun to wear on them all.

The Valentines had stayed at Velma's too for a few days after the fire, but they decided to look for another place, since Hank couldn't be definite about when the burned house would be repaired.

Actually the repair on his house was the last work of that sort Hank had done for a while that year. His co-worker Calvin had introduced him to a friend, Mac Davis, who wanted to start up a soul-food business. Hank had talked to Davis several times. The proposition had sounded interesting. Davis would put up all the money that was required to set up the business. He already knew of a place on Blackston's main shopping street that had most of the needed equipment. Hank would run the place, cook, serve, clean up, and be there whenever the shop was open. The food shop would sell fish and chicken and biscuits that would be prepared daily, greens, beans, sweet potatoes, pie, and soda. Sometimes there would be other items such as barbecued ribs, depending on the market price and demand. Davis would be paid a sum each week toward his investment, he and Hank would be paid a salary, and the profit would be divided among the three of them.

Bernice was enthusiastic about the plan. It appealed to her sense of improvement. Hank would move from the position of a paid worker to that of a businessman/manager. What Bernice and Hank did not know at that time but, Hank mused, had certainly learned later was that the restaurant business, including carry-out food shops like this, were marginal and highly likely to fail. The success of those few small independent places that existed in an area like Blackston was probably due to the other activities carried on there. These places sometimes served as a center or front for gambling or narcotic sales. Some bought liquor and resold it at a higher price on Sunday and during times when liquor stores and bars were closed.

Another thing that Hank and Bernice had no way of knowing until after they had committed their aspirations, energy, and ready cash to the business was that Mac Davis rarely wanted to do what they thought was a fair share of the work. Most often he didn't work in the shop at all. But he did come around at the end of each day to check on the proceeds and at the end of the week to receive his "return on investment," no matter how the shop had done. After this payment, there was often no profit at all.

These were things that Hank and Bernice became aware of after they had involved themselves for fourteen- to sixteen-hour days, six days a week, trying to make money in the soul-food business. Not only Hank and Jack but also Uncle Jonesy and Bob's two young boys, who were visiting from the South, had worked in the shop. The shop had been open from noon till past midnight hoping to catch the lunch, dinner, and late-evening crowds during the warm months.

As Hank sat on the porch looking back on the experience, he told himself in hindsight that his own eating habits should have warned him that the business would fail. Hank liked home-cooked food, he liked to eat it at home, and he didn't like to spend a lot of money on it. Although the shop cooking was quite good, it cost more. The Blackstonians Hank knew didn't like to spend their money on restaurants and bars. Almost all cooking in the community was done at home. Food was prepared at home even to take on long car trips to the South or to take to formal dances in the city. Drinking, too, was almost always done at home. Occasionally people were willing to pay by the drink at a party, although even on such occasions many brought their own or drank before coming, and rarely was drinking done in bars. Hank was aware of only four bars in the entire community, and two of these were technically outside the borders of Blackston.

Hank nodded to Uncle Jonesy, who had come to sit on the porch with him. He reminded Jonesy that they had often grumbled together about the food business while they worked there. Uncle Jonesy suggested that businesses that were part of larger chains and that required a larger investment than a Blackston resident could afford might be successful. He was thinking of Kentucky Fried Chicken, which had just opened a shop at the busiest intersection in Blackston. A few food businesses, such as the Chinese restaurants that were in the area before Blackston became Black, seemed to do well. But Jonesy and Hank agreed that they had learned the hard way about small food businesses.

The Wilsons had decided after a few months that they were putting great amounts of time and energy into a place that some weeks was not even earning their salaries. Up until then they had felt that the shop's location on the far end of the shopping area was only a minor disadvantage that word-of-mouth advertising would overcome. But this didn't happen, and things didn't look as if they would change. Now the two young boys were going back down South to attend school so they wouldn't be available as free labor, and Bernice was tired of running a household on such unpredictable funds. She refused to touch the amount Hank knew had been saved when they had repaired their own house in the spring. Bernice was very serious about moving to a better area.

After the food shop had closed down, Hank had found a job as a construction laborer. Russ, who had moved into the first-floor apartment in the two-family house where the Valentines went after the fire, had been working for a construction company for many years, and he got Hank the job. The wages were good, better than what he had been paid for installing paneling and tile. The one thing Hank didn't like about the job was that it often required him to work on projects in different areas of the state. He might be at home only on weekends. Unlike Russ, who liked the money and liked to gamble and party and drink, Hank preferred to be around his home and family.

It was while Hank was on one of these out-of-town jobs that Randy was killed. Hank's brother Jack had been sitting on the porch, right where Hank was sitting now, when it happened. Jack had been talking with Randy a short time before and had watched Randy going in and out of the building next to where he lived. He had seen a Black man he hadn't recognized as a Paul Street resident go rushing out of the building. But it wasn't until he saw the police cars pull up to the building that Jack realized something had happened. Then he saw two cops carry out a Black male figure propped up in a chair. By this time an ambulance had arrived too, and the body was transferred to it. The cops in the second and third police cars began pushing people away. Jim B. and his wife were put into the back of one police car. Plainclothes detectives arrived, and there was much activity across the street. The rest of the story they heard from Jim B. when he came back from being questioned at the police station.

Just sitting here thinking about it made Hank sad even though it had happened some time ago. From what Hank had heard, it had been Randy's fault too. Nobody blamed it on drugs. Hank had only to think about his own brother Jack, who had been an addict most of his adult life. Jack didn't get into that kind of trouble. And Jim B. was a steady user and still going strong.

As Hank saw it and discussed it with Jonesy, some people knew how to handle dope and some didn't. A good example of someone who didn't was Clara, the transvestite, who had taken an overdose of heroin and had been found by his grandmother, curled up dead in his own bed. She had told people he looked as though he were sleeping. According to the gossip on the street, Clara had tried the stuff only once or twice before. And there he was dead and only a teenager.

There had been at least two other violent deaths on Paul Street since the time of the fire. The hard-working, respectable, and seemingly successful Mr. Gardner, who mopped sidewalks and ran a food business out of his basement, had shot a man who was coming out of the Gardners' own house. And the seemingly shy, non-English-speaking wife of Mr. Rodriguez had stabbed and killed her husband during what she described as a family quarrel. Mr. Gardner was in jail. His family continued to be a part of the community, as did the Rodriguez children, whose mother had been freed.

People died and were killed here often. Miz Rosalie Newman, for instance, had died of a heart attack. But Hank agreed with a number of people from the block who felt that the welfare system had killed her. Miz Newman had had ten children of her own from two marriages, six of them under ten years of age. Then an infant grandson arrived. Rosalie Newman and her aged mother cared for all of them. Then the doctors told Miz Newman that her heart condition, high blood pressure, and diabetes would not improved under this workload. The social worker at the Jewish hospital clinic where Miz Newman had been receiving treatment helped her to appeal to the welfare department's social-services division to secure a household helper.

Hank knew about this part of the case because Miz Newman had asked Bernice to help her in appealing to the welfare department. Miz Newman needed to have the welfare provide payment for a woman who had agreed to help with the supervision of the children and with the housework. Bernice had told Hank that the welfare's response had been to offer to take the ten children and distribute them among foster homes and to the city shelter. After first offering to help her get a homemaker, the caseworker began to insist that this was the only solution possible. The doctor's order that Miz Newman cut down her work activities became the basis for arguing that she could not be a competent mother in her condition. Rosalie Newman became so agitated at what seemed to be a forced breaking up and dispersal of her family that she had a heart attack and died.

When Hank thought about things like that, he felt that groups like the Black Panthers might be right after all. Hank had never picketed or demonstrated in any way, but he had let the Panthers use his basement for a fund-raising party once. Now the Panthers weren't active around Blackston any more and he didn't live here either. But nothing seemed to change.

Hank and Uncle Jonesy sat and smoked a little of Jonesy's grass, watching the afternoon slip by and each thinking his own thoughts. Hank turned to Jonesy and continued out loud a conversation he had been having with himself. Hank needed to work out in his own mind why he felt so comfortable in this community. It wasn't the police or the hospitals or the fire department, and it certainly wasn't the sanitation department or even the supposed community organizations like the Blackston Community Council that he appreciated. It wasn't even the place as a physical place. His new house was nicer. And Blackston as a physical place might not exist much longer. Several buildings had been torn down on Paul Street alone, just since Hank had moved. Even the abandoned house next to his own, which had stood empty and gutted since the fire three years ago, was supposed to be torn down soon. At this rate the entire community might be wiped out, as the planners predicted.

What Hank liked abut Blackston was the people. They worked

hard and played hard. They were friendly and ready to share. Where Hank now lived the houses were a little nicer and newer, and in some cases the rents weren't as high as here in Blackston. Hank knew this from comparing the rent he paid with what he received from the two families in his Blackston house. But the people where Hank now lived had succeeded somewhat, and they wanted to forget what it meant to work and not succeed.

Hank's own house-hunting and house-buying experiences had made him aware that there wasn't enough money or enough places for all the people in Blackston to run away to. He knew that he had been able to leave Blackston because he was young and lucky, pushed by an ambitious wife, ready to try any work and any moderately safe hustle. This was combined with a welfare stipend to his wife and two welfare rents paid to himself as a landlord. A spell of illness or an investigation by the welfare department might end all of this any day.

AUNT BEA COULD TELL that Bernice was pleased with herself. Bernice for her part was sitting near Bea's window feeling happy with the world, talking a little loudly and joking. Bernice had enjoyed gossiping with Bea when they both lived on Paul Street. Now she could enjoy the feeling of success at having gotten away and still keep up with the people and events that interested her most. Bernice had been sitting here drinking vodka and grapefruit juice for some time. John, Bea's husband of six months, had retired to the bedroom after the first hour. He was new to Blackston and didn't know many of the people they were talking about.

They had been talking about Paul Street residents past and present. Aunt Bea described the new people who had moved onto the block, the babies born since Bernice left, and who was now seeing or living with whom. This gave them both a chance to express their pleasure, surprise, or scorn. This was the first time that Bernice had had a chance to talk with Bea at length, although they had seen each other many times since their move. In fact, Bernice not only had come back for Bea's recent wedding but had been the maid of honor. Bernice had handmade Bea's formal gown as well as her own floor-length, powder-blue gown. It had been a small but very successful event. Aunt Bea's son, who had been in the hospital for two separate operations on the leg he smashed in a motorcycle accident and who had been immobilized for months, came for the affair. The Valentines also returned to Blackston for Aunt Bea's wedding.

Their talk gave Bea a chance to ask about Bernice's sister-in-law, Velma, who had also moved from Blackston and was living with Bernice and Hank in their new home. Bernice protested that she would stick to the facts since she wasn't sure why Velma did what she did. Bernice had seen the change coming ever since Velma's first husband, the father of Georgette and Marisa, had come back to Paul Street after being let out of prison. He arrived just after Velma and Steve's newborn baby, their second and her fourth, had died an unexplainable crib death. Within a few weeks, when Hank and Bernice asked Velma to join them in the two-family house they planned to move into, it was Velma and her first husband who came. Steve, who had lived as Velma's common-law husband for some seven years, had left. Bernice didn't want to talk more about it. She seemed to feel that anything else should be said by Velma. Aunt Bea only prolonged the topic long enough to add a few comments of her own, since she knew both men. Then she and Bernice agreed that it wasn't their place to judge.

Bernice switched the conversation over to Bea's own family or at least Bea's brother-in-law, Oscar. Bernice wanted to know more about what was happening with Oscar. His fall had occured before Hank and Bernice left Blackston. Aunt Bea described the hospital stay and Oscar's permanent job loss. As far as Bernice could tell, Bea switched back and forth between being sorry for Oscar and being angry at him for what she saw as his failings. She complained that Oscar was now back to drinking, even though he had had no alcohol for months after the accident and his return home from the hospital. And she felt that he had been stupid to stop taking the physiotherapy sessions. Bea admitted that Oscar looked more ghostlike and seemed more purposeless each day. Not even the trips to the South to stay with his sister had helped. Oscar's sister had a sick husband who needed company in the house while she worked, and both families felt that this would give Oscar something to do and a change of scene. Oscar went

South twice but quickly returned, and nothing seemed to help him adjust to being unemployed.

Bernice looked out the window and across the street to where Hank was still sitting on the porch of their old house. She decided it was about time to rejoin him and think about making the trip back to their new home. She noticed that Aunt Bea seemed to be having trouble keeping her eyes open. Bernice got up and began saying goodbye. It seemed clear that Aunt Bea's protests were purely form and that she would probably join John as soon as Bernice left. As Bernice went out the door, she realized that she too would be the subject of gossip sometime in the near future. Bernice felt sure that when this happened the talk would be largely positive. As Bernice saw herself, and hoped others saw her, she had been more successful at doing those things that everyone else in Blackston did too.

Bernice worked, occasionally in an office, always in her home, but she worked hardest at keeping Hank working too. She received her welfare payments, dealt with the welfare department and the caseworkers, and even arranged to receive welfare-subsidized rents for their old house. And last but not least, Bernice knew that she had hustled—buying "hot" goods, selling commercial products, playing the numbers, giving card parties and dances. Bernice and other Blackstonians found all this acceptable and indeed necessary in order to make it.

THE MEANING

ANY CONCLUSIONS a social scientist derives from data must be based on a number of factors. Among the most important are (1) the researcher's biases and view of the world and (2) her academic training and expertise in the use of research tools. These two factors are combined when the researcher reviews and evaluates prior work in the field, thinks of questions to be asked, observes what is out there, and analyzes what she sees. The introduction to this book offers the reader some insight into my social and educational background, my previous work and social-action experience, and my biases as I know them. In the preceding sketches of community people I have presented some of the reality of Blackston as I saw it played out in the lives of people I knew well for five years. Here I want to discuss some of the questions that were in my mind when I went into Blackston. The following comments seem to me to flow from the data. Each point will refer to the data for support.

There is no denying that there is drug addiction in Blackston, as well as alcoholism, temporarily female-headed households, welfare, and hustling. But to ignore the wider social system within which these responses develop is to be lured into the view that the individual's actions are responsible for rather than a result of the present unequal position of Afro-Americans in American society. To ignore the variations within individuals over time, the variety within any family, or the shifting combinations within the community leads to an image of sickness endlessly repeated. In reality, within the cycle of change for individuals and within the family and group, there are also long years of steady employment, stable families, males in the home, sobriety, and freedom from drug addiction. There are also disastrously high unemployment and underemployment and inadequate welfare support. Finally, the American success dream, rarely realizable in the ghetto, is still strong enough to keep Blackston people hustling.

That poverty exists and persists in Blackston is indisputable. The income figures quoted earlier show that Blackston residents are in the lowest income range in the city, and that the area has the highest fire rate and the highest rate of tuberculosis and other diseases in the city. Housing is in extremely poor condition. It would be possible to detail many other features that make Blackston typical of the worst big-city ghetto-slum areas in the United States. Yet most people in Blackston, like the Burtons, Wilsons, and the Wards, continue to live in the area. Even those few Blackston families that are financially able to move to an area of the city that is in better physical condition are often kept from doing so by racial discrimination. A Paul Street couple, friends of the Burtons, the Wards, the Wilsons, and the Valentines, had been able to buy a small frame house on a small lot in a mainly White community only a few miles from Blackston. They had painted the house inside and outside, making the trip from Blackston each day after the man's regular job was finished in order to do so. They were aware that their new neighbors-to-be were not happy to have them move in. This first became apparent when all the windows in the house were broken during the night when the house was empty. But the Blackston parents persisted because they felt that the neighborhood and schools in this new area would be better for their children. They repaired the windows. Then the house was burned to the ground. This family gave up their attempt to move and were still located on Paul Street when we finished our study.

A personal experience early during our stay in Blackston convinces me that this kind of discrimination is strictly racial and in no way related to the presumed characteristics of people on welfare or other personal habits or character. Six months after we began our work we received funding from a government research agency and were able to hire a secretary. We wanted her to be located close to but not in the area where we were working. We therefore asked our White landlord and his wife (who had been born in the very building where we now lived in Blackston and with whom we had good relations) to rent us an apartment in a building they owned in a mixed community on the western border of Blackston. They refused to do so, stating very explicitly their view that if they allowed one Black person to live in the building—no matter what the individual's economic or educational level—White tenants would move out, and they would be able to have only Black tenants thereafter. In Blackston they had less choice. We did not point out to them that, unlike our later three assistants, this secretary was White. We did resolve to find other housing in Blackston for ourselves, preferably something owned by community people. And we did add to our knowledge of the outside forces that keep Blackstonians down.

Early in our time on Paul Street we became aware of the great human effort that people in Blackston put into making their situation as good as possible. In addition to regular jobs—often very dull and low-paid work such as janitorial jobs, dishwashing, clerking, housecleaning—many people spent their evenings in such activities as dressmaking or service-car driving to supplement their incomes. Mr. Gardner, for example, worked in a janitorial job during the day and as a watchman part of the night. In addition he organized a club intended to raise money by charging admission for entertainment events, and on weekends he sold liquor and fried foods from his basement. Early in the morning, before going off to the first of his jobs, Mr. Gardner would take care of the property he was buying. One of my favorite photographs of the block shows Mr. Gardner mopping down the sidewalk in front of his house.

Not every person in Blackston was as full of energy or as conventionally respectable as Mr. Gardner, but still much hard work went on. Johneva Burton worked full-time as a clerk in a supermarket during the day; at night she hustled stolen items to support an addiction to heroin. Her heroin habit was time-consuming in itself. First she had to make the money and then she had to make a connection with a drug dealer. Beside a heroin addiction and a full-time job, she cooked and kept house for her father and her children. In addition she dealt with the welfare bureaucracy—also an extremely time-consuming activity. A visit to the welfare offices began with a trip of several miles on public transportation, usually at 7 A.M. so that one could be near the beginning of the line. If one was lucky enough to get inside the front doors that day, he or she would often wait for hours to see the person to whom the case was assigned. Sometimes the applicant was then sent from one part of this multifloored office building to another to wait or to some other social-service agency in another part of the city. Frequently the bulk of a working day was taken up with welfare. And the best return that could be hoped for was less than $2 a day. Welfare is indeed hard work.

Despite their scant resources, Blackstonians put a lot of work into making their lives as pleasant as possible. It is in this respect that they differ most obviously from many people in other communities. People in Blackston would often spend what I considered large amounts of hard-earned cash on such luxury items as stereo phonographs, which could be used for family entertainment or group parties and dances. Hank, the Ward sons, and several other people on the block owned stereo sets with enough volume to provide music for the entire block, as they often did during a block party or other community activity. People in Blackston, no matter what their age or income level or income source, like to entertain and give parties and cook for company. This last feature ranged from daily cooking that could always feed unexpected guests to party cooking—fried chicken, ham, sometimes spareribs and fish, rice, greens, beans, and often cornbread and iced cake. Women would shop and cook all day in order to party at night. National holidays—particularly Christmas, New Year's, Memorial Day, Fourth of July, Labor Day, and Thanksgiving—were always an excuse for celebrations, as were birthdays and weekends in general.

Some people might characterize such lavish entertainment in the face of limited resources as improvident and likely to keep people from saving enough to escape from the slum. Yet the amounts of money spent could not really make a difference in the basic circumstances of inadequate housing, racial discrimination, limited job opportunities, poor city services, and all the other things that Blackstonians escape from, at least temporarily, through dancing and partying. The social life of Blackston, willingness to share, free and easy access to whatever liquor and food there was among friends, neighbors, and kin are the features that those who moved away commented on most often and said they missed.

If there is any reason to believe that the music, eating, drinking, and sharing are part of an overall life style that keeps people in Blackston at the bottom of the economic and social ladder—and there is no way to show that this is true—I believe that Blackstonians would choose to retain these features at almost any cost. This is an important part of their life style, consciously cultivated and much appreciated. During our five years in Blackston it became an important relief to us also after a week of dealing with businesses, shops, landlords, police, schools, welfare, and the general problems of living in a ghetto slum. On Sunday evenings there was little or no partying because people had to go to work on Monday morning. But on Friday and Saturday nights, Paul Street and the many other streets in Blackston would have parties where one could drift in, survey the crowd, dance, play cards, drink, or otherwise join the party or move on. For us such activities were an important way to see material conditions and social life.

Another feature of Blackston social life seems to be, if not peculiar to such an area, at least importantly different from the ideals expressmd by the wider society: Blackston families often differ from the two-parent-and-children unit so commonly accepted as proper. In Blackston a household usually consists of two parents and their children, but it may also include grown children by previous matings, adult brothers and sisters of the parents, grandparents, and sometimes nonrelatives. For example, Clara Haynes moved in with the Wards for several months after she left her parents' house, and Aunt Bea provided many months of temporary refuge to a homeless young adult male. When this man was not staying at Aunt Bea's, he lived in the home of his sister on the same block along with her husband and children.

In Blackston family life is organized and supportive. Households are often adapted to externally imposed conditions. The people who make up these units give each other emotional support while sharing material goods. Thus Thaddeus Burton Jr. and his wife are able to hold down full-time jobs while raising two young children because they share an apartment with her parents, who provide many services, including child care (that is, love, discipline, and instruction, as well as food and clothing). In turn, the parents are supported, in part, by their daughter and her husband, and their joint apartment is the headquarters for Miz C's numbers-writing activity. A similar child-care arrangement involving both her parents and her sisters and brothers allows Brenda Ward to hold down a full-time job. And Little Ann, the mother of Edward's first child, became a part of the Ward household and remained so long after Edward had moved out and married another woman.

Child care is probably the primary need that activates the mutual sharing of psychological and material resources. But many other situations also prompt such sharing. During the emergencies following the fires at the Wilson house, kinsmen took in not only all of the Wilson family members but even the tenants. When Mother Wilson came north for an operation, three separate households—Hank and Bernice, Velma and Steve, and Uncle Jonesy—combined to provide food, driving services, hospital visits, company, and general psychological support.

A feature of family organization that is often cited as especially characteristic of Black people and Black communities is the female-headed household. In Blackston we found such households *not* to be very common. For reasons related to welfare eligibility, such households are often overreported to welfare workers and other official collectors of statistics. Work, welfare, and hustling must be combined in order to secure a minimum level of income for poor Black families. Welfare is not available legally to mothers and children who have an employed or employable male in the household. Therefore men in Blackston avoid being reported to the welfare department and are often "missing" when outsiders compile official records, take surveys, or complete censuses. Women and children help to hide the men, who are often working, hustling, and functioning as husbands and fathers. Men of all ages go unreported, but young adult males who are hustling, avoiding the draft, or anxious to avoid official scrutiny for a multitude of reasons make up an especially large proportion of the "missing" men reported by the census analysts, the Urban League, and others interested in Black community statistics.

Likewise, the apparent high rate of illegitimate births among women on welfare is largely a function of the legal requirements imposed for receiving welfare aid and the resultant reporting procedure. For example, all of Darla's children, Brenda's twins, and Hank and Bernice's daughter Tylee were born to women wrongly listed on welfare roles and therefore on hospital records as "never married, abandoned, or divorced." Unmarried mothers, illegitimate births, and households with no functioning father do exist in Blackston as elsewhere but not to the extent that popular prejudice, welfare statistics, or survey data indicate.

Of the eight women in the Burton, Ward, and Wilson extended families receiving welfare aid, seven had husband/mates with whom they shared their homes and their welfare income. This means that records showing fatherless households are inaccurate for seven out of the eight cases in this sample.

Darla was legally married to and living with Randy. Thaddeus's wife was employed as well as married. Brenda Ward was also employed and legally married. Little Ann was not legally married but lived in the Ward household, where her child's father, Edward, was present during most of this study. Bernice Wilson was legally married to and living with Hank. Velma lived with Steve during the five years of this study and rejoined her legal husband when he was released from prison. While Velma received welfare support, at no time during this study was she an unmarried head of household. Even the two remaining cases had men in the home. Gloria received home-relief payments because her husband, Oscar, was disabled and living at home. Johneva, who was not married, lived with and kept house for her father as well as her children.

Another popular image of Black Americans is that they constitute a self-perpetuating core of welfare recipients whose parents were and whose children will continue to be a burden on the state because they have not learned the value of work. Yet among the welfare people in these typical Blackston households this was not the case. Darla's mother had worked at a hospital job for many years to support her family after her husband was killed. Randy's father had never received welfare assistance and had worked for over two decades at the same job. Neither Gloria nor Oscar came from a welfare-supported family. Brenda's and later Edward's use of welfare pre-dates their parents' application. And Gloria and Oscar were forced to resort to welfare for support only after Oscar's twenty-five-year employment ended with his accident. Their eldest son has never applied for or received welfare support. Velma and Bernice, who made such effective use of their welfare income, did not learn this behavior in their respective homes, since Mother Wilson and Bernice's parents did not raise their families on welfare. Mr. Wilson worked at a variety of jobs available to a Black male in a small southern town, and Bernice's father worked in a steel mill in the northern town where Bernice was born and raised.

There are many people in Blackston who are reluctant to use welfare as a source of support. Gloria Ward, for example, turned to welfare only in desperation, after living and raising a family for a quarter century on job earnings. There are others, like Little Ann, who come from nonwelfare families but who learn early that welfare is one of the few sources of support available to a teenage mother who dropped out of high school. There are also people in Blackston whose parents received welfare before them. But there were no people among the hundreds we knew during our five years in Blackston who existed on nothing but welfare or who wanted nothing more than welfare or who were content with the result. Because of the low level of welfare payments and the individual's desire to do better and have more, most Blackston welfare recipients combined their welfare payments with jobs and hustling of various kinds. This very combination is illegal and subject to penalty—but to be willing to make do with welfare alone is considered degenerate. Thus welfare recipients are in the bind of being damned if they do and damned if they don't.

Most people in Blackston were raised in families that share the popular negative views of welfare recipients. They are constantly kept aware of such views through radio, television, and newspapers. Similarly, most Blackston residents experience conflict between the values of the wider society, which they by and large accept, and the day-to-day needs of ghetto living. This situation often leads to open disputes among people or to conflict within the individual.

The lengthy and heated discussion that Aunt Bea, Gloria Ward, Bernice Wilson, and their men had about stolen goods was a particularly clear case. Everyone agreed that stealing is wrong and should not be condoned, rewarded, or encouraged in the young. Yet the two sisters reacted differently in applying this norm to a concrete situation.

The total behavior of the individuals at the dinner party was not unusual. Blackstonians often make explicit statements of norms and values and discuss at length the implications of the behavior required or prohibited as it affects their lives. Their commitment is more than verbal. Many of them act in terms of these stated values much of the time. Or, as in the situation described here, some individuals behave in ways consistent with the stated norm even though they lose some immediate advantage. Others go against the norm but rationalize their choice by pointing to a conflicting ideal, such as their obligation to provide basic necessities for their children. In the discussion described it was possible for individuals to make different choices and continue to interact comfortably.

For Hank Wilson and his wife, Bernice, the conflict is not so easily resolved. Both are committed to the ideal of a conventional two-parent family headed by a working male. In keeping with this ideal, Hank has been a steady worker. He does not approve of the welfare portion of their combined income, even though it enabled them to buy a house and move away from Paul Street. In fact, he would like to do without welfare as a source of income. Hank has made this point many times to Bernice, sometimes in the presence of others. One of his stated reasons for rejecting welfare is that he sees it as a constant reminder that he cannot support himself and his family with his own skill and initiative. By conventional standards it is a sign of emasculation. Yet Bernice is even more committed to the conventional ideal of upward social mobility, which is possible only with money. She therefore will not allow them to give up welfare as a source of income. Hank's own commitment to the male role ideal and his resulting sense of continued failure become an unresolved internal conflict.

Many Blackstonians subscribe personally, verbally, with mixed feelings, and with varying seriousness or sincerity to conventional middle-class, Euro-American (mainstream) values. They as well as social scientists might see a distinction among their neighbors between the "working poor" and the "undeserving poor," or between "mainstream" ghetto dwellers and "typical" ghetto dwellers. Yet in reality each individual and family tends toward one or the other side of this distinction at one or another point in time. Any individual may move back and forth between these categories depending on the relative importance of various sources of income and associated life styles.

Value-laden terms such as "unworthy poor" or "typical ghetto dweller" are not accurate descriptions of a community like Blackston. Because of the changes that occur over the lifetime of an individual in Blackston, sometimes over brief time periods, such a dichotomous model is not only arbitrary but unproductive as well. If one also considers the variety of behaviors practiced within a single family, the model becomes meaningless. Even the activities of most individuals at any particular point in time overlap such a distinction.

For example, in addition to the variation within the Burton extended family in the period described here, there have been changes over time in the primary source of income and associated behaviors of each of the individuals. Up until the time he was sent to jail, Thaddeus Burton Jr. had combined a life of hustling, drug use, and no conventional job with being a husband and father. For more than three years after being released from prison, until the time of this writing, he has been steadily employed, no longer used drugs, and continued as a husband and father.

Thaddeus's sister Johneva, who also was addicted to heroin, combined a job in a supermarket with hustling to support her drug habit. At the time of this writing, Johneva is no longer employed and no longer uses drugs. With welfare support, she keeps house for her three fatherless children and her steadily employed father.

Randy Burton was an active drug addict until the time of his death. Thus three of the four Burton children were involved with drugs at some time in their lives. To guard against assigning too much importance to drug addiction as a determinant rather than an effect, and to show the folly of assigning these individuals to a category based on this characteristic, it is only necessary to consider the case of their father, Thaddeus Burton Sr. Here is an individual who is part of the same extended family, who has an education beyond high school, a long, steady work history, no record of trouble with the law, and no drug or alcohol addiction, and yet the same need to combine work, welfare (through his daughter Johneva), and hustling (mainly his recreation of gambling at cards) in order to have a life only marginally different in other respects from that of his children.

Alcohol addiction is another characteristic often used as a criterion by users of the worthy/unworthy model. Within the Ward family, it was the steadily employed father whose alcohol consumption was very high. Yet it never interfered with his work life until the drink-induced accident that ended his long working career. His wife, Gloria, drank alcohol only on special occasions. Gloria's sister Bea, who drank heavily for years, no longer drank at all after her marriage. And there was no alcohol or drug addiction among any members of the second generation of Wards.

The same mixed picture emerges when one considers such items as legalized marriage, the legitimacy of children, and all the possible combinations of work, welfare, and hustling as sources of income. It is more reasonable, accurate, and insightful to recognize that most, if not all, residents of an area like Blackston are forced by circumstances to practice a combination of these patterns.

Each of the three extended families described here exemplifies the need, in an economically depressed, minority community such as Blackston, to combine income from jobs, welfare, and hustling in order to maintain even a low standard of living. Even this combination does not provide for economic security or mobility. Thus within the Burtons' extended family, Thaddeus Sr. has been employed for decades at the same job; Randy and Darla have hustling and welfare respectively for their primary source of income; Thaddeus Jr. and his wife, Renée, have both been steadily employed for years at low-paying conventional occupations, while she also receives welfare and he hustles as much as possible. They live with Renée's father, a steadily unemployed Black male, and her mother, who writes numbers. Randy's unmarried sister, Johneva, receives welfare payments.

Oscar Ward is actively committed to conventional employment as the proper way to support his family. He does not reject hustling, but he has never been successful in using it as an additional income source. His wife Gloria does occasional domestic work, sells commercial products such as Avon and Tupperware, and buys and sells "hot" goods to supplement their resources. She was finally forced to apply for and live on welfare after Oscar's accident. Their oldest daughter, Brenda, has been steadily employed for at least eight years as a low-paid clerk in an insurance office. At the same time, she has been receiving welfare assistance. After her marriage, she continued to work and to receive welfare while her husband was employed in a supply house. Her brother Edward worked for some time at the same kind of job in the same company where his father had worked for twenty-four years. Perceiving such employment as futile, Edward at the time of this writing had chosen to shift to a job as a service-car driver, which offered the possibility of combining work and hustling plus mobility, and a choice of work hours. Legal earnings in his new job are no higher than the factory pay, but the possibilities of earning more on the side through hustling appeal to Edward, who now has four children to support. It was through the mothers of his four children that Edward was involved with welfare as a partial source of support.

Bernice and Hank Wilson combined these varied sources of income most successfully. Hank worked steadily at a variety of jobs, including the management and co-ownership of a small business during the five years of this study. At the time of writing, he is employed as a carpenter. Bernice received welfare support prior to and during this study and continues to do so. During this same period she has been at various times unmarried, married to Hank, temporarily employed, and constantly hustling through such activities as hosting weekend gambling games and card parties, working with the Cameo Club, and buying and selling "hot" goods.

Despite the large amounts of time and energy that go into all these activities, no one is secure. Within the Ward household, Brenda, a high-school graduate with a white-collar office job, welfare support, and a working husband, is only marginally differentiated from other Blackston residents. For her the combination of two adult incomes and welfare does not provide a level of living much higher than that of her parents, Oscar and Gloria, who live in the same type of apartment in the same building along with other people whose main source of support is welfare or hustling. The money Brenda was able to save before her marriage was used for furniture. Beyond these possessions, Brenda's material surroundings and life style are not much different from those of most people on Paul Street.

No household of the Burton extended family has much in the way of material possessions, though there are some differences. The furniture in Thaddeus, Renée, and Mr. and Miz Jay's shared apartment was much newer and of better quality than that in Randy and Darla's apartment. Darla Burton is able to feed and clothe her three children and maintain an apartment only by supplementing her welfare check with money earned selling marijuana and in other minor hustles. But because such additional income is unpredictable, even so basic an issue as whether there will be food for everyone toward the end of the two-week welfare-check cycle is not assured. Thaddeus Jr. and his wife, who are steadily employed, have more and better clothing to wear to work than Darla and Johneva. Yet Thaddeus Sr., who also goes outside the Blackston community to work, dresses no better than Randy, his addict son. And the children in the three households are all well dressed when sent to school. Each member of the extended family lives in a similar low-income area. Their individual responses to the basic problems of earning a living and surviving in such an area have not produced any marked differences in life style.

Although Bernice and Hank have used their combined resources to move out of Paul Street, they have only been able to move into another ghetto area, and they remain totally vulnerable to the shifts in fortune that often affect other Blackston residents as well. If a fire occurs in their Blackston house, they will lose the rent from their welfare tenants, which enables them to pay the mortgage. After paying off the mortgage, they will probably not be able to get fire insurance at all. If the federal government cuts back on its support of poverty programs, which seems highly likely at the time of this writing, Hank will lose his current job. If the welfare department makes an investigation into either Bernice's or Velma's case, they not only could lose that source of support but would also be open to prosecution, jail sentences, fines, and the possible loss of both houses.

There are two more general points to be made about the problems of a community like Blackston. The first is that individuals soon discover that their own sophistication and ability to manipulate others provide only limited returns. This is related to the second point: basic problems in such a low-income community are built into the entire structure of American society and cannot be changed by individual manipulation.

At the start of the fieldwork I assumed at a subconscious level that my college education, well-developed verbal ability, knowledge about the larger social system, and middle-class social skills and style would enable me, unlike many ghetto residents, to handle successfully any problem resulting from the impact of the larger society on my family, myself, or any less-skilled ghetto resident I chose to help.

This assumption was proved totally wrong many, many times. I exercised my greater expertise, I shared my knowledge with others, I learned from ghetto residents an assertiveness that I had lacked, and still this combination was ineffective. The problems I faced in Blackston, described here in terms of the individuals who shared them with me, do not stem from individual actions or lack of action. The problems of employment, education, health care, housing, welfare—of making the system work—are structural and institutional issues whose solutions are beyond the individual. Their resolution must involve massive change in society.

The American economic system as it is currently organized leaves a significant portion of the population periodically or permanently unemployed. Because of racism, most of the men and women in Blackston who are able to find work are limited to marginal, fluctuating, low-paid work. At the same time they are required to pay high rents for substandard housing and inflated prices for low-quality food and consumer goods.

They are also surrounded by professionals external to the community whose pay is high and whose positive contribution to the community is low. For example, a policeman, a fireman, or even a garbage collector earns three times the legal minimum wage paid to many Black workers in the community. Yet police services are repressive, fire protection is brutally destructive of already scarce property, and garbage collection often produces filthy conditions on Blackston streets and lots. Among professionals, social workers and teachers in Blackston earn three to four times the wage of community people. But in Blackston welfare services are inadequate and the educational establishment is ineffective. Many, if not most, of the professionals working in Blackston are arrogant. Encouraged by social-science thinking, which is often laced with hidden value judgments, and the popular press, they stereotype the people in communities like Blackston as being from welfare-supported, broken homes characterized by no interest in education, no family life, emotional instability, deviance, and so on.

There is little or nothing an individual can do against this array of forces. Individual solutions are often creative and require a great expenditure of time and energy. Combinations like jobs, welfare, and hustling allow the individual to survive. Yet the total supply of available resources remains the same. Today I hustle you. Tomorrow you hustle me. Individual manipulating does not make for any change in the basic situation. The problems are social rather than individual and require massive social solutions.

OTHER VIEWS

THE PRECEDING MATERIALS were gathered through ethnographic observation and participation in a single low-income Black community between 1968 and 1973. When we went to live in Blackston, there were few studies of Afro-Americans that involved researchers as participant-observers in the communities under study. This was true despite the fact that many social scientists, including anthropologists, spoke and wrote about Black culture, lower-class culture, and the culture of poverty among Afro-Americans. The lack of inside data about Black people did not prevent many anthropologists from making statements about and taking strong positions in regard to the Afro-American poor in a way these same scientists would find totally unacceptable if the subjects were some exotic unstudied people far from American shores.

What are ethnographic techniques and why was such methodology not applied to Black communities within the United States? Basically ethnography is the study of a whole culture, society, or community. Ideally the ethnographer attempts to define the limits of the society/culture, to explore its content, and to identify the points and ways in which the society/culture is related to other units. To do this the ethnographer (1) employs various forms of verbal interaction or interviewing to elicit cultural data in verbal form from members of the group or community under study. The ethnographer (2) collects evidence of cultural patterns by observing directly the ongoing social behavior of people in functioning communities. Ethnographic research involves the investigator's extending his or her direct experience of the social order by (3) participating in the daily affairs of the people who make up the unit of study.

These three broad categories of the technique may be combined in different ways. Emphasis on one or another type of approach varies with the research problem and with the personal predilections or talents of individual researchers. *The crucial quality of ethnographic method is that all three ways of gathering data are employed together so that each may serve as an independent check on the others.*

There is no reason intrinsic to the methodology itself that should exclude Black communities from ethnographic study. Instead, academic politics, prejudice, and the ease of access to other forms of data have been important factors in keeping anthropologists from doing participant-observational work among Afro-Americans.

Sidney Mintz, in his foreword to *Afro-American Anthropology* (Whitten and Szwed 1970) notes that "fieldwork among Afro-Americans was not the way to get ahead." He suggests, further, that "it can be embarrassing to defend the values of one's informants, when those same informants are members of an oppressed minority, while the ethnographer—like it or not—is a member of the oppressing majority."

One of the best-known figures in anthropology, Margaret Mead, made her prejudices explicit in 1969 in response to a plea for research among the Afro-American poor, who had not yet been studied using proper ethnographic methods. She wrote:

> The anthropologist who lives with a primitive people adds his respect for their way of life to that of the people he studies. *The poverty version of a modern culture contains many elements which require repudiation rather than respect;* shared repudiation becomes inevitably partisan and requires involvement, an application of anthropology rather than pure research. Where primitive people's dignity is enhanced by objective research, "the poor" often feel further demeaned [*Current Anthropology* 1969: 194; emphasis added].

Census data, police and court records by race, welfare-department statistics, school records, and survey materials have long been available for Black communities in the United States. Because such data already exist and represent hundreds and thousands of person-hours of work and tens of thousands of dollars that the researcher needn't expend, social scientists have long used such materials to the exclusion of other kinds of research.

Social scientists have probably most often used census data attempting to describe and analyze Afro-American communities.
Yet there are two important reasons why one should not offer or
accept census data uncritically. The first reason concerns the
figures themselves. The following account by a Census Bureau
staff member should help make clear the "gross inaccuracy of the
Censuses, even during the modern period, especially pertaining
to Black and Puerto Rican and Chicano people" (Aptheker 1974:
16).

The Bureau of the Census, acting as collecting agent for the
Bureau of Labor Statistics, provides national statistics on
unemployment through a monthly survey of about 35,000
households. Jacob Siegel, a staff assistant in the Bureau of the
Census, estimates that such surveys miss 17 percent of non-White
males fourteen years old and over and 9 percent of non-White
females in this age group. In the decennial census of 1960, 25 percent of non-White males twenty to thirty-nine years old were
among the persons who failed to be counted (that is, who were
totally absent from the survey). Siegel goes on to discuss the possible effect of this undercount on the accuracy of such
characteristics as unemployment.

> It is mathematically conceivable that these effects could be quite
> large. For example, consider a group of non-White males where
> 25 % of those who should have been were not counted. Suppose that
> among those who were counted 10 % reported they were
> unemployed. Suppose, further, that all of those who were not
> counted were unemployed, then the true proportion unemployed in
> the total group would be 32.5 % rather than 10 % [Siegel 1968: 5].

In our own work in Blackston, in a comparative study of
underenumeration and related problems, we found

> an undercount amounting to 17 % of the ethnographically defined
> sample population. This magnitude of overall underenumeration is
> more than twice as high as the 8 % error which official estimates
> suggest was the level of net understatement reached in the national
> census of nonwhites by 1967 (Siegel 1968: 25, 41). While the two sets
> of data from Blackston show discrepancies within all age and sex
> categories, by far the major difference applies to males 19 years of
> age and older [Valentine and Valentine 1971: 4].

Why, then, do social scientists use the census? A writer interested in the question of social statistics as the basis for the popular view that Afro-Americans are a small and weak minority has this to say about the census:

> One [factor] is the census—which to secular America is like the Bible—it's something you have to believe in because it's the only thing like it, every ten years and there it is, it's got all the data in it. . . . In any case, the whole point about the census being a basis of truth needs to be seriously questioned, if for no other reason than the white people who run it said it was messed up [McWorter 1969: 66].

The reader is also referred to a number of social-science discussions of the problem: "Needed Improvements in Census Data Collection Procedures with Special Reference to the Disadvantaged" (Lee 1968); "Procedural Difficulties in Taking Past Censuses in Predominantly Negro, Puerto Rican, and Mexican Areas" (Pritzker and Rothwell 1968); "Completeness of Coverage of the Nonwhite Population in the 1960 Census and Current Estimates, and Some Implications" (Siegel 1968); and "The Census: What's Wrong with It, and What Can Be Done About It" (*Trans-action* 1968). Because of these kinds of issues, census data should always be presented as approximate and subject to considerations of objectivity, comprehensiveness, validity, and reliability.

A second reason to be cautious in using or accepting census-type data concerns the misuse of statistics to make causal explanations. Census statistics in themselves reveal nothing about culture or about social issues. For example, studies of census data demonstrate clearly that residential segregation of Whites and non-Whites in the United States has increased over the last few decades (Taeuber and Taeuber 1965), but tell us nothing about the social or cultural causes of the changes. Statistics about female-headed households or children under eighteen not living with both parents tell us nothing about the social processes that go on within or between such units. Such statistics do not tell us anything about parental discipline or intergenerational communication. Yet the Moynihan Report on the Negro Family (1965), which is based only on these kinds of data, makes the following social and cultural analysis: "At the heart of the deterioration of the fabric of Negro society is the deterioration of the Negro family. It is the fundamental source of weakness of the Negro community at the present time"(Moynihan 1965: 5). We reject this analysis and similar causal explanations because the data on which it is based are inadequate to support such a conclusion.

When census data are used in this report, they are presented only to convey a general picture of such matters as community size or official unemployment statistics for comparison with other communities. We hope that this brief review of some of the issues surrounding the presentation and use of census data will help the reader to keep an open and questioning mind about the precision of such materials.

Interview data are equally inadequate unless systematically checked against independent sources of evidence. Included here in the term "interview data" are sociological questionnaires, genealogical methods sometimes used in isolation by social anthropologists, clinical and other types of in-depth and open-ended interviewing, collections of autobiographies, and such technical refinements of the interview approach as projective tests. No matter how useful these techniques may be for other purposes, taken alone they cannot produce answers to the questions we are asking or to those asked by other ethnographers of Afro-America. The basic weakness of all interview data is that they consist only of verbal testimony or self-projection by respondents or subjects. Without independent evidence it is impossible to know how such data may be related to the actual behavior of respondents or to the social processes and culture patterns that condition group behavior.

Politics, prejudices, and the tempting ease of access to statistics and other interview data notwithstanding, participatory research has been done, albeit in a partial or incomplete way, by at least a few researchers.

Thus while other anthropologists of the period were studying colonized peoples outside the borders of the United States or the oppressed but "exotic" American Indian, a Black woman, Zora Neale Hurston, applied participant-observation techniques to the study of American Blacks. In 1935 she published a collection of rural Southern Black folklore entitled *Mules and Men.* Her knowledgeable accounts of hoodoo ritual have been attributed by her teacher, Franz Boas, to the fact "that she entered into the homely life of the southern Negro as one of them and was fully accepted as such" (preface, Hurston 1935). Unfortunately, no broader ethnographic report of this work was ever published, and Hurston left the field of anthropology to become a novelist.

From the time of Hurston's book until we were well into our work in Blackston, about a dozen studies of Afro-Americans appeared that can be compared with ethnographic research as described here. Rather than present these studies chronologically, I shall answer specific questions related to the methods used, the population studied, and broad statements of result.

Ethnography provides a means of exploring a way of life by direct, intensive, personal exposure to the conditions of existence within the group. Since the ethnographer attempts to encompass all major aspects and dimensions of that existence, it is important to know how complete the coverage has been in any particular study. Did the researcher immerse himself or herself in the community on a full-time basis? Did he or she interact with members of the group of both sexes and of various ages and degrees of status, marginality, representativeness? How many people were included? Over what period of time? What areas of behavior and thought were observed and /or explored?

Often the answers to these questions are not given explicitly when the ethnographic data are presented. Sometimes the answers can be found; sometimes only guessed at. In the few studies on Afro-Americans that are explicitly labeled ethnographies or that talk about culture as a totality, there seems to be a wide range of answers to these questions.

Francis Ianni did not do any ethnographic work on his "ethnography," *Black Mafia* (1974). Unlike the other White authors described in these pages, Ianni *assumed*, "I could be certain of hostility and perhaps outright refusal on the part of the Black and Puerto Rican communities, to say nothing of the organized crime groups themselves, to be subjected to such a study" (1974: 16). He therefore recruited eight Black and Puerto Rican ex-convicts and trained them for two weeks (!) in observation and recording techniques. Then he "explained the concept of ethnic succession in organized crime" and the recruits began to give him "examples of its reality out in the streets" (1974: 344). If one ignores the self-fulfilling prophecy aspect of this way of organizing a study—the matter of respondents or interviewers giving the project director what they think or know he wants—there is still little match between Ianni's data and his analysis. Ianni frequently refers to his earlier study of an Italian-American crime family (*A Family Business: Kinship and Social Control in Organized Crime*, 1972) with whom he spent three years. This is in great contrast to a secondhand, eighteen-month study of Blacks *and* Puerto Ricans/Hispanics *and* organized crime.

The title of Arthur Hippler's book, *Hunter's Point: A Black Ghetto* (1974), suggests a total community study. Yet it soon becomes apparent that the book is based on four months' field evaluation of a community-organization project funded by the Department of Criminology at the University of California and a year and a half of "further investigations," none of which apparently involved any ethnographic technique, such as prolonged, uninterrupted total immersion in the community. Hippler's study is based on isolated interview data unchecked by direct experience of the social order through participation or even observation of ongoing social behavior of the people as a functioning unit. In a "Short Note on Methodology" (1974: 10), Hippler, who claims to "distrust questionnaire responses," says that in place of questionnaires he elicited life histories, personal sketches, and TAT responses from people at Hunter's Point. Yet a questionnaire by any other name yields the same ethnographically unsatisfactory results.

Roger Abrahams does not call his work an ethnography, but he nevertheless uses it as a basis for making generalizations about Black culture on such diverse topics as life style, self-image, male-female relations, world view, and riots. Abrahams, an anthropological folklorist, is author of *Deep Down in the Jungle: Negro Narrative Folklore from the Streets of Philadelphia* (1963) and *Positively Black* (1970). While gathering data for the former book, Abrahams stayed in an apartment in the Philadelphia ghetto, where he tape-recorded young Black males. His work has limited value as ethnographic description because, even though he resided in the area, Abrahams chose not to participate in the life of the community to any extent beyond using his apartment as a place to record verbal activities such as insult competitions and joke and storytelling presentations. Yet his generalizations about Black culture are not similarly limited.

Urban Blues (1966) by Charles Keil is not presented as a standard ethnography—that is, the study of a total culture—but the author does claim to deal with culture in the popular sense of "the music scene," "soul," and "male image/role." His techniques of data gathering closely resemble ethnographic techniques. They involved traveling with and around blues people, watching performances, talking with performers, and asking questions. Although one gets a sense that his involvement was intense, there is no indication that it was prolonged or uninterrupted or involved systematic observation of the ongoing social life in a total community. Despite the circumscribed area of contact Keil describes, he too makes generalizations about culture in its broader sense.

Hortense Powdermaker's ethnographic coverage is more mixed. She did a study among small-town Blacks in Mississippi in the mid-1930s. Her ethnographic data and analysis appeared in a book entitled *After Freedom* (1939). A very readable description of her entry into the community, her perception of her role in this segregated society of the thirties, and other theoretical as well as personal issues related to fieldwork appear in *Stranger and Friend: The Way of an Anthropologist* (1966). Powdermaker, in keeping with the oppressive White mores of Mississippi in the thirties, decided that she could enter the Black community only in a partial way. She lived in a boardinghouse in the White section of town and ate her meals there. Her nonresident ethnography involved trips "across the tracks" to visit with and interview Black people during regular working hours and trips to Black churches every Sunday, sometimes followed by Sunday dinner in a Black home. In addition to these limits on her participation in the total life of the community, her introduction to the community may have had certain biasing effects, since her original contacts are described as "upper class" and "closest to me in background."

Another limit on her community study is best told in her own words.

> I could not be a participant-observer in certain areas of Negro life, such as the Saturday-night parties in the "flats," the poorest and

most disreputable section of the community. Heavy drinking, gambling, and fighting prevailed at these parties. It would have been clearly unwise for me to have attended them. The Negroes would have been extremely embarrassed by my presence and the whites would have known about it since a white policeman appeared on the scene when the violence or noise was greater than usual. My presence would not have been condoned [Powdermaker 1966: 181].

Because of her evaluation that being a participant-observer in certain areas of Negro life would be "unwise" or "would not have been condoned," Powdermaker limited her own ability to engage in a fully rounded participant-observation study of a Black community. Yet her own experience in a Nashville night club, in which she was obviously a full participant, suggests that her apprehensions may have been unwarranted:

One evening I went to a Negro nightclub in Nashville with three of the younger members of the department, and to my surprise no one at the club seemed taken aback at a white person's being with Negroes and a white woman dancing with a Negro man. One of my friends explained that everyone thought I was a Negro. . . . This was my first experience with unconsciously "passing" [Powdermaker 1966: 135].

Some twenty-five or thirty years after Powdermaker's work in Mississippi, two studies were done by White males among southern urban Afro-Americans in the nation's capital. In *Soulside: Inquiries into Ghetto Culture and Community* (1969), Ulf Hannerz specifies that he also did not live in the community under study. Instead he was in the community only at selected times, "afternoons, evenings, and weekends." This is partial ethnography, leading inevitably to omissions and distortions of data.

Elliot Liebow's *Tally's Corner* (1967) was part of a larger study of Black child-rearing practices in the Washington, D.C., area in the early 1960s. Despite his extensive description of his research techniques, Liebow refrains from acknowledging that his is a "partial ethnography" in the sense that he did not immerse himself in the lifeways of his subjects, night and day, uninterruptedly. Throughout the study, Liebow resided in a Washington suburb and nightly returned to that base and to the personal/emotional ties and time demands of that split existence. This point becomes important when one tries to determine whether the absence of family ties that Liebow noted among his street-corner men is a reflection of reality or an artifact of his study style.

The materials presented by Liebow and Hannerz leave the reader no way of knowing how much the authors may have missed that could be of basic significance. For instance, Liebow and Hannerz, both highly trained anthropologists using essentially similar methods, carried out their research projects within a few years of each other in the Black ghetto of the same American city. Yet they came to quite different conclusions on the crucial question of cultural distinctiveness. When one reads and compares these two works, the basic questions of the existence and nature of any distinctive Afro-American culture remain neither convincingly resolved nor satisfactorily transcended. More progress toward answering their own questions could have been made had the researchers committed themselves to living with the people they sought to understand.

If the investigators maintain their residence outside the community under study, focus much of their personal existence elsewhere, and participate actively in significant institutional involvements outside the locale and social setting of the fieldwork, both the data-gathering ability of the researcher and the quality of his or her experience are radically limited.

Another limitation of Afro-American ethnography is the tendency to focus on very small social units. Liebow studied a single network of street-corner associates. Hannerz confined his work to one residential block. Although both studies present some rich and suggestive material, they represent only fragments of the social wholes that are relevant to the questions asked.

Within a street group or a block of households there is only a narrow range of social situations, institutional frameworks, and other settings for behavior. The ethnographer who confines himself or herself to such units has direct access to only a fraction of the actual world of the people being studied. He or she may not see the wider activities, beyond household and street life, that make up a very significant part of social existence, and may miss most of the major economic, political, religious, and service institutions that impinge upon people's lives, including kinship, associational, and other informal and small-scale interactions and relations beyond the immediate unit of study. For all these enormously important aspects of life, such researchers are largely confined to the evidence of volunteered or elicited verbal testimony. In this respect, the researcher is again working within the limitations of interviewing, unchecked by observation or participation.

Washington, D.C., in the 1960s and early 1970s was a popular locus for social-science studies of the people who were crowded into our nation's capital but were somehow not a part of it. In most cases the studies were of Blacks, but *Hard Living on Clay Street: Portraits of Blue Collar Families* (1973) is about White people. It is noted here because the families described in this book by Joseph Howell are in many ways strikingly similar in behavior and attitude to Blackston people.

Although Howell is a city planner by training and admits to only a few courses in sociology and anthropology, he moved into the area of study with his wife and child and did a participant-observation study for one year. It is evident from his writing that the family's participation was full-time and total during this period.

Virginia Young, a White anthropologist, does not claim that "Family and Childhood in a Southern Negro Community" (1970) is an ethnography, but she clearly used ethnographic techniques. Young's method of research was to "observe and record in detail the behavior of parents and children in their own houses and yards" (1970: 270). Young states in her abstract: "The American Negro family is generally interpreted ethnocentrically, as an impoverished version of the American White family entirely on [the basis of] clinical methods of research" (1970: 269). She uses the ethnographic technique of observation and participation to show "highly distinctive behavioral styles, some of which have remained undiscovered by psychoanalytic studies and others of which differ markedly from the extrapolations of clinical research" (1970: 269).

It should be pointed out that Young's study was done in a southern community of under 10,000 persons. It would be hard to demonstrate in a definitive way the relationship of this community to the large urban populations covered by most of the other studies reviewed here and to "Blackston." With this consideration in mind I nevertheless point out that many of the people from Blackston were born and reared in similar southern communities, return often for visits and extended stays, and sometimes leave their own northern-born children with southern relatives for the summer or during crises such as school strikes in the North. As part of our study we made a number of trips with Blackston residents to communities such as the one described by Young. On such visits we lived with friends and relatives of Blackstonians for up to a week or more. On the basis of these interactions, I feel strongly that Young's study population and ours have many important similarities despite the differences in location and group size.

In *All Our Kin: Strategies for Survival in a Black Community* (1974), Carol Stack has made a contribution toward exploring and elucidating the kinship networks of poor urban Blacks that is comparable in importance (though even more extensive in detail) to the work Young did in describing child-rearing practices. In the mid-sixties, Stack, then six months' pregnant with her first child, entered a midwestern community of 50,000 with the help of a woman who had grown up on welfare in the Flats, as the area was called. This woman introduced Stack to two unrelated families, one from Arkansas and one from Mississippi, and from that point the researcher was on her own in getting to know people, living with them, and learning their way of seeing things. She became a part of several networks of people, joined them in their daily activities, and organized her entire life and work within the community.

In addition to duration and intensity of involvement (that is, whether the anthropologist is available at all times of day and night, whether she merely "visits" informants or brings them into an office for interviews or develops social and emotional ties based on shared living) there is also a question of the completeness of the ethnographic sample in terms of age, sex, and similar factors. Often authors make generalizations about all Blacks, or Black family life, or Black culture on the basis of quite small or sex-bounded groups. A review of the ethnographic work on Afro-Americans reveals some striking examples.

Arthur Hippler's own assertion is that the group he chose for investigation was "probably *not typical* of San Francisco blacks—perhaps not even of all Hunter's Point residents" (1974: 5). Yet a page later he states, "Though this is a select population . . . [they] constitute a fairly accurate picture of the condition of much of America's black population." In fact, Hippler first describes the community as consisting of some 10,000 dwelling units and 50,000 people, then specifies that he had close personal ties with four families. He continues, "I do not feel I truly became part of the community" (1974: 7) and asserts no claim to "understanding" the quality and meaning of life in Hunter's Point; yet he states, "My investigations were essentially in the area of uncovering dynamics and personal and social structure which, by and large, appeared to me to be pathological" (1974: 9).

If Hippler's lack of integration into the community, lack of understanding, and nontypical sample have not convinced the reader to reject his conclusions and generalizations about Afro-Americans, a description of his investigatory techniques should. Hippler, an associate professor of anthropology, discusses his study methods in the following terms: (1) "some techniques cannot be described"; (2) a "high-status technique involved such tactics as appearing to be so involved in talking with the 'important' people . . . that 'ordinary' people could afford to ignore one's presence"; (3) "on the other hand, a drunken bum sprawled out in a doorway or sleeping in a bar is nobody to present the 'special' self to. In early stages of my work, and especially on Third Avenue, I often wore very old clothing and in fact did present myself in these situations as a non-communicative and uninvolved 'bum' "; (4) "finally with some few people, I was able to make clear that I was an ethnographer" (1974: 9). Serious students willing to credit the study population with a modicum of intelligence and sensitivity must question the value of such "ethnography."

Ianni's generalizations about Black and Hispanic cultures and crime are not supported by the behavioral data presented in his descriptive sections. The Blacks and Puerto Ricans described as ethnic successors to the Mafia on the basis of this ethnography consist of: (1) a single Black pimp and his four or five prostitutes, (2) a Black man in the numbers racket in an area described by

Ianni himself as still controlled by Italians, (3) a cleaning-store proprietor/fence and the three drug-addict/shoplifters with whom he works, and finally (4) the gypsy-cab industry. Ianni states that his data on gypsy cabs "are not proposed as 'typical' of the range of gypsy operations, criminal or otherwise, nor do they in any way represent a statistical average of what gypsy cab networks are all about" (1974: 258).

> It is worth noting the various criminal activities that Superfast and its drivers get involved in, ancillary to the fundamental illegality of gypsy cruising. Herminia Rivers, a prostitute, often uses Superfast cabs to get from one assignation to another, *because* she lives in the Superfast neighborhood and *because* she considers the Superfast people, in contradistinction to Yellow Cab drivers, "one of us." More seriously, Robert Murphy is a heroin addict and a small-time pusher who occasionally horse-hires the cab of Frank White in order to peddle drugs out of it. White is aware that Murphy pushes *but does not know the use to which he puts the cab.* On the other hand, he should be able to guess [Ianni 1974: 262; emphasis added].

This level of data is then organized under the emotion-laden title *Black Mafia: Ethnic Succession in Organized Crime.*

Deep Down in the Jungle is based on interview material supplied by young Black males. This narrowly selected and limited population excludes the many older and younger men in the ghetto, as well as women and children of any age group.

Further, Abraham's study is based on the use of verbal interview responses only. In an extended critique of the relationship between Black studies and anthropology, Charles Valentine describes Abraham's work in these terms:

> The book conveys a strong feeling that what one is seeing in its pages is a partial picture viewed as youthful street men might see it. Perhaps to some extent it is a picture presented as such young men would wish an outsider to see them and their community. . . . A body of folklore may be like a sacred book or a great ideological statement. . . . These same bodies of words can say many different things to different listeners or readers. There must be some attempt to understand the source as a whole and in its own terms. . . . If the meanings of verbal creations and expressive culture more broadly are really to be clarified and illuminated, it is necessary to inquire into how they are related to the concrete actualities of existence [Valentine 1972: 18, 19].

Powdermaker's ethnography, *After Freedom*, was one of the earliest Afro-American community studies. As we have noted, the author lived outside the community, was introduced to the community by upper-class people, and admittedly avoided situations involving the poorest and most disreputable section of the community. Powdermaker also admits that adult Negro males, children, and adolescents are not represented in her data at all except as described through her female informants. Nevertheless, she expresses her confidence that her sample eventually included all social groups. One could wish for more evidence that it did.

Tally's Corner deals specifically with street-corner men. Liebow points out that his study covers only some two dozen men, and he himself questions "to what extent this descriptive and interpretive material is applicable to streetcorner men elsewhere in this city or in other cities, or to lower-class men generally. . . ." (1967: 14).

Most of the data in *Soulside*, Ulf Hannerz's study of Black families, were gathered in a single block of a Black community of Washington, D.C. Hannerz is not so modest as Liebow about the generalizability of his materials, although he is quite candid about his bias in favor of "differences" between Afro-Americans and others. He states an interest in what he terms "ghetto-specific" modes of action and goes on to say, "This does not necessarily mean that [ghetto-specific modes of action] are all unique to the black ghetto, nor that they occur there with greater frequency than mainstream oriented acts." He specifies that "all ghetto dwellers will not get equal time here. . . . There are people in the ghetto who have good, stable jobs, help their children with their homework, eat dinner together at a fixed hour, make payments on the car . . . to their largely mainstream way of life we will devote rather little attention" (1969: 15–16). Thus Hannerz tells us that he did not go into the ghetto to observe and record and analyze the actual range of social and cultural patterns or way of life there. Instead he went to find "differences," and he specifically ruled out recording or analyzing "similarities." It seems a clear case of self-fulfilling prophecy on Hannerz's part to conclude, as he does, that Afro-Americans do indeed have a "ghetto-specific culture."

Black males have been the focus in most anthropological

studies as well as in many sociological and psychoanalytic works, particularly those dealing with deviance, delinquency, the male role, and conflict between male and female in the ghetto. It is refreshing to find in *All Our Kin* a look at the Black scene from a woman's point of view. Stack's closest associations were with women and their families. But like Young, who was interested in the behavior of parents and children, Stack also observed and interacted with men.

From such a point of view, Young and Stack are able to make generalizations about families—men, women, and children. Among Young's findings is that in the vast majority of families she studied, males support their families and play an important role in the family. "At the same time there are many illegitimate births, multiple sequential marriages, and frequent dissolution of marriage" (1970: 272). Stack's work probes more fully into the way in which these characteristics are played out in the daily existence of people from the Flats.

Afro-American communities are not tiny, isolated societies. Most Black people in the United States grow up in two worlds in a number of ways. The educational system and employment generally take them outside their community or otherwise bring them directly into contact with the White mainstream world, even if they live in a segregated ghetto area. Any experience with welfare, hospitals, the police, the courts, or social-service agencies almost always takes place in the larger American society. In addition, the media, particularly television, bring mainstream images, values, language, and behavior into Afro-American homes continuously. This is not to say that there are no institutions or behaviors that are unique to Black people or at least are more widespread within Black communities. Expressive styles, both verbal and aesthetic, entertainment, many social events, churches and clubs, recreational activities, and organizational activities like that involving the Black Panther party or similar Black groups may allow or encourage or necessitate uniquely Afro-American styles of behavior or organization. Language may also be influenced by the need to understand and communicate in two distinct ethnic/social worlds.

This process whereby Afro-Americans grow up with dual competence has been described by Charles Valentine (1971: 32–34).

Biculturation is important here because anyone attempting to describe the Afro-American world must be aware of the constant impingement of the institutions and influences of the wider American society on Black people. Do the works we are reviewing here demonstrate recognition of these influences? Again the answer is quite mixed. In most cases Afro-Americans are treated as a separate, self-contained, isolated group rather than as part of the wider American society.

Powdermaker, who lived in a situation where the wider American society strongly limited even her research design and must have been extremely oppressive in relation to the Black community in Mississippi in the 1930s, offers little institutional analysis. Powdermaker was well aware of the segregated school system imposed on the Black community. She describes Black teachers forced to beg White administrators for their salaries and White policemen who patrolled the Saturday night dances in the Black community. Yet she treats the Black community as a self-contained unit and does not explore the restrictive impositions by the school system or the police.

Keil's discussion of Black culture and mainstream institutions is more confusing. For example, in a section in which he attempts to deal with analysis and prognostication he presents such unqualified assertions as "Negroes are the only substantial minority group in America who really have a culture to guard and protect" (1966: 191). Keil then describes "slum conditions, welfare colonialism, foul schools" as institutions that "constitute the perpetuative core of Negro culture as it exists today" (1966: 192). Thus he designates an externally imposed condition as the "perpetuative core" of Negro culture and then suggests that Blacks should guard and protect this culture.

Hannerz specifically chose not to investigate the nature of relations between Afro-American culture and general American culture by ruling out of consideration all those people whose bicultural competence produces what he terms "similarities." Thus he concentrates on small-scale interpersonal relations and puts forward as a listing of Black culture traits the following: domestic dominance by women; a male role focused on toughness, sex, and alcohol; the battle of the sexes; fear of trouble in the environment and from people; interest in music and religion; hostility toward the White establishment. Hannerz thus ignores most of the complex daily interrelationships between Black people and their environment.

Hannerz's incomplete picture contrasts with Liebow's analysis of similar street-corner men in the same city at roughly the same time:

> The streetcorner man does not appear as a carrier of an independent cultural tradition. His behavior appears not so much a way of realizing the distinctive goals and values of his own subculture, or of conforming to its models, but rather as his way of trying to achieve many of the goals and values of the larger society, of failing to do this, and of concealing his failure from others and from himself as best he can [Liebow 1967: 22].

Carol Stack provides a critical analysis of the relationship between Black communities and the wider society. Particularly in the concluding chapter of *All Our Kin* she integrates her data into an analysis of the larger social system, which provides the framework for intergroup relations in the Flats. She combines concrete description of human lives with penetrating analysis of the economic and political setting of Afro-Americans.

Howell's *Hard Living on Clay Street* distinguishes two separate life styles, which he called "hard-living" and "settled-living." Superficially they are similar to Hannerz's "ghetto-specific" and "mainstream" behavior styles. Unlike Hannerz, however, Howell does not ignore either style but rather sees them as representing

> two opposing pulls or forces many people in this community felt throughout their lives. Caught between these two pulls, some people tended to shift dramatically from hard living to settled living and back again. At one point in a person's life he or she might be extremely hard living, at another a very settled person. . . . Often it was extremely hard for a person to reconcile these two opposing forces. Within a given family some brothers or sisters pursued one course of life, some another [1973: 7].

Howell's description of the lives of Clay Street residents and their integration into the wider social system demonstrates that a nonspecialist can sometimes present a more balanced study than some of the trained ethnographers whose work on Afro-Americans is reviewed here.

The following chapter will show how our own research was planned and conducted so as to avoid many of the problems of the literature reviewed above.

THE DESIGN

WHEN MY HUSBAND AND I entered Blackston in the summer of 1968, we were aware of what we saw as shortcomings in previous ethnographic work. We felt that most social-scientific work on Afro-Americans suffered from using the wrong methods and asking the wrong questions. Previous studies had applied ethnographic methods incompletely to a large, complex urban group that was integrated at many points into the wider structure of the entire American society. We also had misgivings about the use of interviews, surveys, and censuses.

In our own work we planned to use such techniques quite critically and only when accompanied by independent checks such as observation, participation, or multiple cross-checking. In designing our research we tried to see that it was not unnecessarily limited in scope, application, or duration. In the process of carrying out five years of research in Blackston we developed two extensions of ethnographic method. One of these is participation from multiple perspectives, which enabled us to expand our attention beyond the narrow community context to the larger institutional setting. The second was involvement of the subjects of study in the analysis and writing up as well as in the collection of data. These activities will be described at length in this chapter.

Ethnographers had long shown that ethnographic techniques could be used to study the social structure or cultural system as a totality. Studies such as Liebow's work on associational networks and Stack's material on kinship networks demonstrate the value of ethnographic technique for the study of limited aspects of larger systems. We felt that if we applied traditional ethnographic techniques in different contexts and from a variety of vantage points, we could address our question directly: To what extent are the conditions of group life due to sources within the group and to what extent to influences from outside?

153

We chose an area that was a named community made up largely of low-income Black people. In addition, the community we chose was removed from our personal and professional ties. In this way we hoped to deal with some of the most important defects in previous work. We cut ourselves off completely from outside demands of a personal or emotional nature and from all academic connections. We spent every hour of the day and night in Blackston. We did not visit our immediate families, other kin, or prior friends, nor did we invite any of them to visit us at all during the first year of the research project. Only after the first year—when we had become integrated into the community to the extent of being asked to join community residents in visits to their kin in other states and countries—did we feel somewhat more free to communicate directly with noncommunity people or have them visit us.

This is not to say that we did not attend social or cultural events in the wider world. Our operating rule was that if any Blackston resident invited us to some extracommunity event, it was acceptable to take part and also would contribute to learning the variety and limits of the life of Blackstonians. In fact, accompanying community residents to work, to social events, to visit kin, or "to take care of business" often took us outside the geographic limits of Blackston.

From our experience in Blackston we feel strongly that a female/male/child team is an ideal ethnographic group. Each member can work more intensively with members of the same sex as well as get a perspective on the same topics from members of the opposite sex, with less danger of the distortion and imbalance we saw in previous work that concentrated exclusively on either males or females. My work as well as my husband's was with both males and females. Because of my previous socialization in sexist middle-American society, I sometimes found it easier to relate to males than to females. Black males raised in an equally or possibly more sexist bicultural world were also able to develop some intense and relatively open relationships with me as a young Black female. If I were to return to restudy Blackston I would—and now feel I could—work at having more intense and more informative relationships with women. There are also situations in which a couple together is the most acceptable unit. Our son, Jonathan, served as an excellent rapport builder and an important part of our research team. Our willingness to allow Blackston residents to care for him and teach him within their framework of rules and beliefs served to demonstrate to many people—beyond our verbalizations—that we had a real desire to learn and respect their ways.

During our work in Blackston we interacted with people from all age groups. Most of our unplanned interactions occurred with those between twenty and fifty years of age. Our recorded life-history materials cover respondents from fifteen to fifty-five. In addition we did a number of substudies that involved specific categories of people, such as a study of feeding patterns of infants and small children, education issues among school-age children and their parents, and a census substudy particularly concerned with young adult males. Thus we avoided concentrating exclusively on adults or any particular age group.

We did not find that race/ethnic-group membership was a hindrance for the Euro-American member of the team beyond some initial suspicion that he was a bill collector or undercover policeman. We dealt with those who expressed these suspicions as we dealt with all Blackston residents who were interested in us, by letting them know we were anthropologists, explaining what this meant and what our study purposes were. We did this many times over, whenever necessary, and we were always totally honest about our institutional connections and finances.

We purposely chose not to be introduced into the community by anyone, hoping to be avoid being placed in a particular category in regard to class, politics, attitude. On our two preliminary visits to Blackston we walked through more than 150 of the 200 blocks in the community. On the second visit we found an apartment in a largely deteriorated, heavily Afro-American section and made arrangements to rent it and move in the following month. On this visit we also met several leaders of the local community council, the umbrella antipoverty agency that represented over 100 organizations in Blackston. One of the most prominent leaders in the council, a long-time resident and activist in Blackston who later became a close and valued friend as well as an important informant, was aghast at our choice of a place to live. She felt that the entire area was in bad shape, but that this particular section was by far the worst.

After having conducted our project for a time, we concluded

that the minimal social field that would be necessary to attempt to answer our questions was what local people themselves call their community. The area has generally understood territorial boundaries. In many respects it is internally divided and disunited. At the same time there are operative structures of community-wide organization, principally focused around a community council. The population of roughly 100,000 is approximately two-thirds Afro-American. There are many varieties and levels of exclusively Black associations and organizations. The community also has a broad array of mainstream American institutions, such as businesses, political clubs, churches, schools, hospitals, and clinics.

ETHNOGRAPHY FROM MULTIPLE PERSPECTIVES.* To do the kind of study we saw would be needed involved tackling a research unit of enormous scale and complexity by traditional ethnographic standards. We developed an approach that may have potentialities for other ethnographers of the Afro-American scene and other settings in complex societies.

The basic operation is to take part in different roles providing multiple observational perspectives. These perspectives correspond to major strategic positions and relationships in the social field, such as welfare client–social worker, patient-doctor, or employee-employer. A brief and simplified example would be to share a community member's role as a welfare client and then a few hours later, as professionals interested in the welfare system, to communicate on a professional level with social workers to get a different perspective on the interaction. We thus found a way to make a simultaneous study-from-within of distinct but interacting organizational and institutional units. The major advantage of this approach is that it transcends the more conventional procedure in complex societies of examining different institutions separately.

We began our work as participant-observers in a residential block and its surrounding neighborhood. We lived in this same block for the five years of the study. Here we concentrated on

---

*This section is adapted from an unpublished paper written jointly by Charles A. Valentine and Bettylou Valentine during the early stages of the Blackston research.

domestic life, socialization patterns, sex roles and sex relations, kinship and associational networks, peer groups, street-corner activities, neighborhood economics, and the smaller localized institutions, such as churches and places of entertainment.

Our participatory approach involved focusing our personal lives quite fully within the community. We began simply as newcomers to the block. Initially we sought contacts with neighbors for the simple information and minor aid a family needs in establishing itself in a new neighborhood. From the beginning we told everyone we met our reasons for being in the community. We immediately began actively sharing with our new neighbors our varied experiences of tenement life, street activities, neighborhood shopping, and so on. This quickly led to home visits back and forth, cooperative babysitting, and then food exchanges. From an early point onward we had people of all ages visiting our apartment every day. We used our car to give many people rides and extended ourselves in this respect somewhat more than other auto owners in the neighborhood. We played what part we could in informal credit networks. When various extralegal bonanzas of goods periodically appeared in the neighborhood, we found ourselves in the networks by which such windfalls are distributed.

Initially there was much curiosity about us, some suspicion, but very little hostility that we knew of. With hardly any exceptions, the hostility and suspicion melted away as people came to their own conclusion that we were in fact nothing other than what we said we were. We built some rapport by taking people places in our car and lending small amounts of money—and refusing to be exploited in these respects. Because of the greater need and hustling skill of Blackstonians, we were not always successful in avoiding exploitation. Our verbal skills enabled us to be useful in such ways as interpreting legal papers or helping with school homework or income taxes. People discovered that we were willing to take part, as ordinary participants, in virtually any neighborhood or community activity, organization, or enterprise—block associations, drinking and gambling parties, protest demonstrations.

Most important, we believe, everyone aware of us in the community knew that we actually lived under the same conditions as other community members. Like everyone else, we were sometimes without heat, hot water, or functional plumbing. We were as exposed as anyone else to the multiple hazards imposed by the lack of police protection and the frequency of police harassment. Our child could have died because of the same combination of incompetence and irresponsibility that caused the death of two babies in the same hospital emergency ward to which we took our son for care on the same night. We could give many more examples. From this viewpoint, most of the anxious debate in anthropological circles about access to Afro-Americans and other Third World communities seems to us largely beside the point.

It was not long before we found ourselves drawn beyond our neighborhood base into the wider activities and associations of our blockmates and other neighbors. We were thus introduced to larger institutions that operated within the community but were controlled from external power centers and were largely staffed by White people who lived elsewhere. These included schools, hospitals, the police department, courts, jails, places of employment, major denominational churches, political centers, welfare agencies, and other social-service establishments. We discovered that it was these institutions that channeled the most direct influences of the wider society onto the ghetto community. It was in these settings that the community members daily confronted the individuals, institutional features, and customary routines of the dominant strata.

The specific process by which we expanded our attention beyond the narrower community contexts to the larger institutional settings is important to our method. At first we accompanied community members through many complete episodes with external institutions. Our role as observers was known to those we accompanied. Especially in our initial contacts, however, we allowed institutional personnel to perceive us merely as associates of the community people in the interaction. Concretely, this meant such procedures as the following: When people were ill or injured, we went with them to health institutions. Then we relied on our status as healthy associates, temporarily responsible for the patient, to stick stubbornly with the individual through as much of the ensuing process as institutional personnel would allow. We joined one public-school parent association with the help of our godchild's family. We later continued to participate when our son became a pupil in this same school. We also participated informally in several other schools. With the help of cooperative community leaders, this provided many opportunities to observe numerous aspects of the educational process, from classrooms to parent-teacher interactions.

We followed individuals as closely as possible through the processes of arrest or complaint to the police, confinement, obtaining counsel, being tried or giving testimony in proceedings against someone else, and the various complications of these events. We visited neighbors or other community people confined in every major penal institution near our area. Accompanying people through interactions with welfare investigators, caseworkers, surplus-food distributors, and various other social-service personnel gave us direct access to the impact of agencies in this field. We took part in the workday of many employed persons whose situation either allows temporary volunteer service, such as many anti-poverty jobs, or makes it possible to tag along informally, as in community political fieldwork. In the role of various laborers, we visited places of employment, such as factory and domestic work or truck driving.

What this part of the method did was to enable us to experience the externally controlled institutions much as community people experienced them. It was, of course, essential that the individuals who took us with them through these experiences were also well known to us in their own domestic and neighborhood settings. This made their observed behavior, their volunteered or elicited explanations, and their expressions of feeling in the external settings much more meaningful to us. Thus, in effect, we had the full resources of sample data not only from informant testimony but also from direct observation and considerable participatory experience covering a very large portion of the community's collective life. The varied sources and kinds of data functioned as mutual checks on one another, giving our findings what we feel is a high level of validity.

The method as described thus far is still quite incomplete. It did not take us long to be impressed by the fact that much in the structure and operations of external institutions is hidden from the worm's-eye view of the community person—be she or he patient, inmate, prisoner, employee, client, or whatnot. If there ever was a situation in which Goffman's dramaturgical analogies hold good, it is here (see Goffman 1959, 1961, 1963). So many vital processes go on backstage that the whole institutional apparatus is simply not intelligible through the community individual's experience alone. Community people do have well-developed ideas of what goes on behind the scenes, but their ideas cannot be proved right or wrong by the techniques so far indicated.

This led us directly to the next and by far the most difficult phase of our method. As participant-observation in the company of friends and neighbors began to show diminishing returns in any one institution or class of institutions, we attempted to gain institutional access at other levels. This involved adopting one or both of two additional roles: (1) scientific observer with official permission to carry out research on the institution from within, and (2) consultant to the institution on matters of community relations. The effort to achieve these kinds of access was enormously difficult, extremely time-consuming, often frustrating, and by no means always successful. We encountered bureaucratic confusion and diffusion of responsibility, professional suspicion and hostility, endless institutional defensiveness, and many other forms of resistance. The early coolness and initial negativism of some community people—even that of the most militant Black nationalists, reacting to us as an interracial couple or as social scientists—was never remotely comparable to the problems created by external professionals and bureaucrats. Presumably, this contrast was due, in part at least, to the fact that we were not full participants in these institutions in the same sense that we were active members of the community. Indeed there is a substantial degree of mutual exclusiveness between these two arenas of participation.

Nevertheless, we achieved some successes in this aspect of our approach, which we feel amply justify recommending the approach to other investigators of the urban scene. In two general hospitals and one mental health clinic we managed to gain considerable freedom of observation, access to medical records (with the permission of the patient), admission to staff meetings, and opportunities to consult with professional and other personnel. In one school district, where the administration happened to be closer to the community than in others, we were officially welcome to study all activities from classroom operations to private meetings and negotiations of the district board. Several major branches of the principal community antipoverty agency accepted us both as participant-observers and as informal consultants at all levels of a variety of activities. The school district and the antipoverty agency were partly special cases, because community leadership had enough influence so that external control of their operations was not complete, as it was in the case of the hospitals. Access to the hospitals was far more difficult to gain.

The means of gaining such access and opportunities were quite varied. They included making contact through community people who had ties with institutional administrations, demonstrating that we had something uniquely useful to offer as consultants, building personal rapport with selected professionals, invoking our own professional status and affiliations, and a great deal of simply pushing our way into institutional settings where we were not initially welcome. Ethnography is not for the timid. In several complexes, including the penal system and the police department, we were never able to exercise this methodological approach.

The focus of our work was always the Afro-American community. Therefore we used our opportunities for data gathering within the larger institutions primarily to understand the processes and experiences through which community members go in these settings. We resisted the temptation to refocus our attention on the institutions as such. We utilized our backstage access to personnel, procedures, and records primarily to throw further light on what happened to individual community clients with whom we were acquainted and to categories of clients we knew were common or important in the community. Thus we learned much about institutional structure and operations, as well as the beliefs and attitudes of institutional personnel, but the frame of reference was always community relations.

The contexts so far mentioned by no means exhaust the types of settings in which we applied this technique. We also observed from multiple viewpoints within the wide variety of community structures where ethnic unity and distinctiveness are vigorously asserted. These include militant and nationalistic political organizations, religious bodies, and forums for artistic expression.

One further feature of this community sometimes made it necessary to add yet another aspect to our methodology. Many Blackston people had close ties with others outside the community, most often because they had come to the community recently from another area. Sometimes crucial aspects of individual or family behavior were not intelligible—either in terms of community norms or with respect to wider institutions—unless one had direct knowledge of these more or less distant associations. In some cases we were able to visit these extracommunity settings—in other areas, cities, states, and countries—for brief observation, interviewing, and participation. Community people accompanied us on such field trips and renewed the relevant ties in our presence. Thus we have been able to add another perspective on the behavior and experience of people who belong to the Blackston community.

It is when these various sources of data are integrated in focusing on a case study or other unit of investigation that their combined potential becomes evident. Consider, for example, the three families described in "The People." They were all in residence on the block before we began our study and they remained there during the five years of our research. During that time we accompanied all the primary actors, both male and female, to their places of employment. We interacted constantly with the Wilsons and the Wards and even more intensively over a shorter period of time with the Burtons. We have interacted with the extended families, friends, and neighborhood associates of all these people. We have been able to see them, not only through the eyes of these others, but also as they were seen and dealt with by sets of employers as well as educational, custodial, law-enforcement, social-work, and health-institution personnel. In turn we know what all these institutional settings and categories of personnel look and feel like to the Burtons, the Wards, and the Wilsons. We traveled to other states with these people, as we did with many other Blackstonians.

The point is not that all this has yielded unusually detailed case histories. It is, rather, that these cases and many like them give perspective on behavior patterns and social settings that are relevant to our basic questions about the impact of outside forces on this community and the sources of Afro-American inequality. Our method enabled us to make an intensive examination, from multiple perspectives, of many kinds of relevant phenomena.

COMMUNITY PARTICIPATION IN WRITING.   When we entered Blackston in 1968, we felt strongly that our work as anthropologists should contribute positively to the community and individuals whose lives we were being allowed to investigate and share. This meant that we should make ourselves aware of community concerns, focus our particular skills on understanding these issues, and work with other community residents on such problems. Our research design was open-ended and flexible so that it could accommodate a range of community interests. While our own academic skills were often tested by community demands and sometimes found irrelevant, our professional standards were never infringed on. For example, as part of the Blackston research we worked closely with Black Nationalists and others on community issues. We retained their friendship and respect even though we refused to participate in a proposed project that we did not feel was professionally good work. Even after this incident they voted to accept us into a particularly sensitive area of the community from which researchers had previously been excluded.

It was an easy move from the conception that we should help the community to the idea that the community could help us beyond being passive subjects of study. We soon convinced many people that they could help us to improve the validity and relevance of our work. We began by simply speaking with community residents about what we saw. Such discussions took place with many different people. The leadership of the Blackston Community Council was interested in the economic status of Blackston residents and wanted to discuss any fieldwork data or analyses that would help them to develop and better administer their antipoverty programs. In turn the community antipoverty organization provided entree to many community groups, contacts with a wide variety of Blackston residents, and information on the community gathered by other methods that could be used to cross-check our developing data. Our contacts were not limited to organizations. Many ordinary community residents would ask about our continuing work. Some people in the community of an especially philosophizing turn of mind would seek us out for these kinds of discussions. We also approached community friends and tried out ideas on them or asked them to read and comment on papers we were writing and publishing while in the field.

At the same time, people—including teenage males, young adults of both sexes, middle-aged women, and older people —would invite us with varying degrees of seriousness to write up their personal lives. On these occasions we usually pointed out that we were interested in the total community and that if the questioner felt she or he could add to our understanding of the area and its residents, we would gladly listen to and tape-record what was being offered.

We became aware through discussions with community residents that Blackstonians were quite interested in their neighbors, their community, and our understanding and interpretation of it. It became clear that this would be a sharing process wherein we could interpret and explain, to community members of different ages and levels of education, social-science concepts about Black people and show their relevance or lack thereof to Blackston as we saw it. Occasionally people would disagree with our interpretations; sometimes they would add examples to those we had. People with whom we discussed our work and shared our papers ranged from political conservatives to Black Nationalists and revolutionaries. Both men and women and people of many ages read our work, as did employed people, hustlers, and welfare recipients.

While in the field we wrote an article (Valentine and Valentine 1972) about the Black Panther party, which had an active branch in Blackston. Before this paper was given at a conference of the American Anthropological Association and submitted for publication, we shared it with the local Black Panther party and with Huey Newton. Newton arranged to have J. Herman Blake, a sociologist who was close to the party, come to the conference to comment and expand on the paper.

We became convinced through these experiences that any further writing we did about the community should be done along with the persons studied. We began to search the social-science literature for examples on which we could base our newly developing effort. We learned of only two studies that involved some interaction between researchers and subjects about the written materials prior to publication.

In the introduction to their book *Africville: The Life and Death of a Canadian Black Community*, Clairmont and Magill state that "groups of relocatees [persons moved out of the Halifax community called Africville] were subsequently reinvolved in reading and criticizing a draft of the present study" (1974: 36). We were unable to find information about what sections of the book were evaluated or about the relocatees' responses and their effect on the final draft.

Elizabeth Bott, in *Family and Social Network* (1971), offers much more information about her project and the prepublication interaction of researchers and subjects. In this interdisciplinary study of twenty families in urban England, only two of the families are written up in detail. Bott states:

> We wrote many drafts before reaching one that was accurate enough psycho-analytically. . . . Once the drafts were prepared, small sections were taken along to be discussed with the husband and wife. . . . All in all, the process [of postwriting interviews and discussions] took the equivalent of one person's working time for more than a year [Bott 1971: 46].

In the Bott study the researchers were not asking for help in developing their data or even for agreement with or evaluation of their interpretations. In their own words:

> Our activities were much more like therapy than they had been in the earlier interviews, for we were trying to help the couples to accept things emotionally. . . . *We were not interested in* changing the couples' anxieties and defenses, or *even getting them to agree to our inferences*. The real task was to help them over the feeling of indignation that outsiders could see or imply the existence of things in them that they thought were concealed [Bott 1971: 47; emphasis added].

Although the material developed and discussed in this book differs greatly from Bott's psychoanalytic work, her conclusions about the prepublication interaction are of interest:

On the whole we feel these discussions have been productive in that much confidential material can be published, the couples' reactions to our interpretations have helped us to revise our analysis at several points, and all four individuals seem to have come through the experience without harm [Bott 1971: 47].

The Bott study team developed a policy for future work, including the idea that it is permissible to publish material about specifically identifiable individuals if the material is innocuous. Because of class and race relations in the United States, particularly as they relate to the economic and social life of oppressed Afro-Americans, none of the information in which we were most interested seems to us to be innocuous. Besides, the subjects—not just the researchers—should make this judgment.

The Bott team further decided that it would be permissible to publish confidential information about specific individuals if it could be so disguised that the people could not recognize themselves or each other. This was not a procedure that I considered for either general or specific information, although other anthropologists claim to have done so. For example, Carol Stack, writing about people similar to Blackston residents in ethnic and class identity, says:

In the life histories presented in this book, a person's job, family size, and the intimate events in life histories have been changed so that no one would be recognizable . . . [and] . . . in order to conceal the identity of the city, the figures have been slightly obscured. . . . Nonetheless, the description depicts the setting, and accurately characterizes numerous other urban areas in the Midwest and the ghetto quarters within these towns [Stack 1974: xix].

I felt that family size, family structure, and interrelationships were all relevant to important points I wanted to make. I did not see how it would be possible to disguise the people enough to make them unrecognizable even to themselves and at the same time accurately illustrative of the Blackston community. I decided to depict the characters accurately rather than develop ideal types or composite figures.

The Bott study group had decided that "if the material is confidential and cannot be disguised, it should be worked out with them [the subjects of the writing] beforehand" (Bott 1971: 48). This is what I decided to do with the Blackston data.

Plans for the current writing involved a limited number of specific individuals and what might be interpreted as confidential information about sources of income, sexual relationships, and life history. I decided to ask the subjects to take part in the development and writing of the text. In order to do this I first wrote up a draft of the text in story form. I changed the names of the individuals, made up abbreviated kinship charts, and organized one-line descriptions of the principal people in each story. These double-spaced, typewritten drafts were then reproduced, and the relevant story was sent to each major character in the three families, along with a cover letter. A copy of the Wilsons' story went only to the Wilsons and likewise for the Burtons and the Wards. No copies were sent to minor characters or to people who were not members of the extended family involved. A copy of the theoretical material and a proposed outline of the entire work was sent along with the story.

The cover letter described the project and explained that I hoped to use the story as an example in a book. I also pointed out that the work might be seen only by the five members of my graduate work committee or might possibly be published sometime in the future. I asked each person whether the portraits seemed accurate and fair. I asked whether the material would be embarrassing to anyone, and I asked for their comments, corrections, elaborations, or any other reaction. I invited written comments and also gave an outline of the days (several weeks in the future) when I would be returning to the community. I specified that I wanted to meet with each person to listen to him or her. I also told each individual the names of all other people who had received a copy of that particular story. In a few cases with especially large numbers of primary actors, I asked individuals to share their copies with other specified persons.

Although each letter contained the same information, each was written in terms of my continuing relationship with that person. For example, my cover letter to Mr. Burton Sr. was more formal than my letter to our godchild's parents. I did not use form letters, because our five years of research did not involve this kind of formalized interview-questionnaire procedure, and I did not intend to introduce such a factor in the writing-up process.

The three separate sections were sent to a total of fifteen main actors:

The Burtons: Thaddeus Jr., Thaddeus Sr., Darla, and Johneva
The Wards: Oscar, Gloria, Brenda, Edward, Ann, Gert, and Aunt
    Bea
The Wilsons: Bernice, Hank, Velma, and her husband

Several members of the Ward family, contacted by telephone on other matters, indicated that they would respond in person when I returned to the community as proposed in my cover letter. In this same phone conversation one of the young adult females, Gert, said that she and her older sister, Brenda, had read the draft and now proposed to write their own story about us.

I did return to Blackston for several days and attempted to see each of the fifteen people to whom the manuscript had been sent. Of the four Burtons who had access to the manuscript, only Thaddeus Jr. agreed to talk about it. He had shared his copy with a friend, who also commented. Thaddeus Sr. sent the message that he did not want to think about or talk about his son's death. Of the seven Ward adults who had access to the manuscript, I was able to talk with five. Oscar and his son Edward were not available while I was in Blackston. Oscar's other son, Raymond, did not read the manuscript, as he was in Thailand, and neither I nor his parents sent him a copy. Of the third family involved, I spoke with three of the four people solicited, and Bernice claimed to be conveying her husband's views as well as her own.

Of the nine people I talked to at length, only one, Gloria Ward, agreed to mail me a corrected copy of the manuscript. The others specified that they were expressing themselves in full in our talks.

In writing this book three questions were most important to me, and I hoped that working with the people about whom I was writing would help me to answer them: (1) Is the thesis of the book correct and relevant to Black people? (2) Are the portraits accurate, interesting, and exemplary of the thesis? (3) Will the subjects of the writing understand and approve?

From the discussions of the drafts, I received almost totally positive responses to the first two points and varying degrees of neutral or negative response to the third. Seven of the nine people indicated spontaneously that they agreed with the thesis. The other two talked about it and agreed on being asked that it seemed true to them. Almost without exception, respondents repeated a number of times in each interview that the facts within the stories were correct in relation to themselves. A number of the less well developed characters, including Thaddeus Jr., Brenda, Gert, Ann, Dee Dee (with whom the Wards had shared their copy), and Velma, specified that they liked or approved of, or at least didn't disapprove of, their own descriptions and had no objections to such material being published. Other reactions ranged from Aunt Bea's initial comment that she had no right to object, though she was obviously angry and personally cold to the author, to Bernice's comment that she had talked to a lawyer and determined that she couldn't keep the material from being published but wanted me to know that she wished she could.

My husband was present during the discussion with the Wards but did not take an active part. I alone talked with the Burtons and the Wilsons. The following is a description of the major specific responses and my own reactions and analysis. The instances where someone objected to a factual detail or incident were generally minor. Some of the examples given below add further information about the person's interests, worries, or view of the world.

Gloria Ward began the interview by stating emphatically that she had never learned about false insurance claims from her employer and had never told me about such an event. When I pointed out that this event was indeed in my field notes, recording an interaction early in the five years that had been repeated to both researchers, Gloria insisted that it must have been a recording mistake. She also insisted that the fire that burned Oscar's car was not arson for insurance purposes but an accident involving spilled gasoline and that he had not been able to move the car in time. This event was described in the draft text, as it had been partially seen by one of the researchers and confirmed by a number of independent observers. Since the intent of the action cannot be proved, it seemed fair to delete this section from the draft text that was first sent to the major characters.

I interpret Gloria's reaction to these materials as an attempt to have the description of an illegal and sanctionable event removed from the written record, since she sees the possible publication as a threat. This incident provides insight into one community resident's self-perception and her desires for self-presentation and safety from potential prosecution, whether real or imagined.

Some of Gloria's other objections were quite trivial in comparison, as shown in the way she phrased them and the lack of emphasis she gave to them. For example, Gloria objected to the description of her buying food before paying bills or perhaps not paying bills at all. Her objection seems related to an internalized mainstream view about what obligations are most important. Gloria's actual behavior often followed Blackstonian survival rules: food for her family came before formal obligations such as rent and utilities. But she did not want this point made for public view.

Gloria's daughter, Gert, called on the phone the day I was to be in Blackston and came back from other business specifically to see me. In response to my questions, she agreed with most of the points made in the text and theoretical material. She agreed to the description of her specific behavior but objected to having her actions described as "teasing." She said that she acted as she did only to "stir people up." I offered to report her response though not to change the text.

These comments were delivered to my husband and myself as we sat visiting in the Wards' kitchen and living room, as we had done so often during the five-year study.

Gloria's sister's reaction was quite different. Aunt Bea was obviously not the same friendly, outgoing person with us that she had been in the past, although she warmed up somewhat after an hour or more of general talking about neighbors and mutual friends. She did not mention the manuscript during this time. When I brought it up, she said in a brief and snappish way that she had no right to object. I waited until her new husband had left the house and mentioned again that I really wanted to know more about how she felt and why, so that I could correct anything that was wrong. She then said that the story was OK, in fact she had laughed over it at first, but then had decided that I made her sound like a drunk. We talked about this, and Aunt Bea seemed satisfied with my suggestion that I work into the text the fact that she has not been drinking alcohol at all since her marriage. This seemed to be true, according to testimony by her sister Gloria and her friend Bernice. In fact, Aunt Bea's change to a working, nonwelfare, nondrinking woman during the two years since her marriage fits my point about changes in life style over the lifetime of an individual.

Aunt Bea then seemed anxious to convince me that she hadn't been very angry—certainly, by her account, not nearly as angry as Bernice. Evidently the two of them had read their separate manuscripts, had not shared them with each other, but had used one of their meetings to complain and express their respective anger.

Bernice Wilson, her sister-in-law Velma, and Velma's husband (with whom she had become reunited since the study) met with me in their house outside Blackston. Velma's husband, to whom I was introduced, was interested in talking to me because of the reaction the manuscript had provoked. He had been in jail during most of the time covered by the Wilson story. He wanted to know whether I had told people I was doing a study; Bernice and Velma assured him that I had indeed done so, many times. His shrug seemed to convey the suggestion that they had been warned and let themselves in for it. His only other question before going back to his second-floor apartment was about why I assigned his real name to Velma's common-law husband. Since this was done inadvertently while I was developing pseudonyms and before I had met him, I agreed to change the name immediately. Velma seemed quite amused rather than upset about this point.

Bernice told me she had gone to a lawyer to find a way to keep the material from being published. We talked at length about why she didn't want it to be published. Bernice had feared that it could be used by jealous and vindictive former neighbors to report her to the welfare authorities or by the welfare department to prosecute her. We discussed whether she would be recognizable to others from the manuscript and agreed that a number of factors would enable people from the block to identify her. On the basis of this discussion we jointly developed a way to change several features for publication so as to further disguise her identity while still keeping the story meaningfully related to the thesis.

Bernice volunteered the lawyer's opinion that either she or I could deny that she was the subject of the story and that the story did not constitute the kind of proof needed by the welfare department to prosecute. During the course of our talk, Bernice agreed to these points but still insisted that she'd rather not have the book published.

We talked about whether the manuscript contained any information not already known to other residents of Paul Street or easily knowable by other means. Bernice insisted that many people thought she was "only shacking up" with Hank and did not know they were legally married. She also felt that some of the economic details of her house ownership were not widely known. We even laughed about an earlier scene when a mutual friend of ours was giving me the material for a kin study and refused to let me put a symbol on the paper for the legally married husband who was standing right there and who was known to many people on the street as her husband. Bernice, who was able to laugh about the other woman, insisted that in her case it was important not to have this material published.

At this point it seemed important to discover what Bernice thought publication meant. She was most interested in knowing where the book might appear. She and Velma asked if it would be available at corner newsstands. When assured that this was unlikely, they seemed relieved. The exchange made clear how different interests affect one's view. From my point of view, corner newsstand distribution would be excellent because it would mean the possibility of reaching the audience I feel needs to read and ponder the implications of the book. Yet Bernice and Velma specified that they wouldn't mind where else it was distributed, even in Blackston more generally, if it could be kept from people on Paul Street and the surrounding blocks.

Hank, whose feelings Bernice said she was expressing, did not want to be the subject of such a study at all. He was particularly sensitive to the material about their welfare income. But unlike anyone else, Hank asked what good for the community it was meant to bring. According to Bernice he had said that if I could convince him it would make a change for the better for individuals or for Blackston as a whole, he might change his mind. Hank, as I had known him during the preceding years, was a quiet, intelligent, socially conscious person. We had often talked with him about our work. When we first moved to Blackston and were more optimistic about the possibility that social science

might have an effect on the political scene, we used to talk to
Hank about informing policy makers and thus influencing the
development of legislation and community-oriented programs.
Since that time I have come to feel that social science reflects
public prejudices and private programs more often than it
precedes them. I think that the Hanks of Blackston have always
known this.

Several hours later, when I left the Wilson household to return
to Blackston, Bernice repeated her comments that the facts were
correct in all but one instance and that since she was sure I would
publish despite her objection, she would help me to correct the
manuscript. The minor factual error was that it had been Steve
rather than Hank who had gone back into the burned-out house
and interacted with the firemen.

My interview with Bernice was the most interesting and
valuable to me. It was a friendly meeting. I may have tipped the
balance a little in this direction by taking with me a bottle of
vodka and a quart of grapefruit juice. We sat around the kitchen
table and talked as we had over the years of the study period. The
discussion was substantive and philosophical. I was convinced
that of the nine people I'd talked with, Bernice and Hank, even
though he was not present, best understood the thesis and the
relationship of their story to the thesis. Yet they were also the
most vociferous about not wanting to be included.

Velma took me upstairs to show me her clean, neat apartment,
and while admitting to and laughing about her messy place on
Paul Street, she said that it had been kept that way because of
Steve, that the Paul Street apartment was not a reflection of her
personality. She and Bernice would talk at length about what was
happening with them and with mutual friends, and then stop
suddenly and say to each other, "Better be careful, Bettylou may
write about this too."

There were also changes that could not escape notice. Bernice
said that she and Hank no longer owned the Paul Street house
where they had been receiving rent from two welfare-supported
families. But her style of saying this seemed to be false. It seemed
to me that she was sensitive about any information she felt would
make her vulnerable and was trying to hide the truth. Our
previous level of intensive friendship made her statement seem

quite transparent. I am convinced that if I had spent a few days living near Bernice and her family our previous open relationship would have been restored.

Bernice and Velma were the most helpful in making suggestions for additional materials. Bernice wanted me to make explicit—at Hank's request, she said—the fact that the Wilsons had saved our lives during one of the fires. Indeed they had, and that was included in their story, but evidently not with the prominence they felt it deserved. Bernice also suggested one or two incidents about the anthropologists, such as a personal argument she had witnessed. In fact, Bernice and Velma pressed for, listened intently to, and discussed at length with me my rationale for not focusing on the anthropologists.

I feel that all the suggestions made by the people with whom I worked were useful, even though some seemed of minor consequence. For example, Gert did not like the name assigned to her. Whether I changed it or not didn't seem very important. But Dee Dee's name was not changed to her real name, as she had wanted, because it would have jeopardized the disguises of others who did not want to be identified. Some suggestions—particularly that I show the anthropologists at work more clearly—were quite useful. I do not feel that any of the suggested changes or additions was meant to be harmful.

The most challenging informant reaction to the writing was Hank's question: What good can come of this work that will justify exposing me and mine to potentially hostile public view? Anthropologists working with "colored peoples of the ghettos [who] . . . are now angry, literate, and politicized . . . [and] no longer awed by the mystique of the white man" (Willis 1974: 147) will have to find a morally justified answer to that question and be able to communicate it to the questioner. Recognition of this problem perhaps will contribute to the design and writing up of other urban studies.

BIBLIOGRAPHY

ABRAHAMS, ROGER D.
1963 *Deep Down in the Jungle: Negro Narrative Folklore from the Streets of Philadelphia.* Hatboro, Pa.: Folklore Associates.
1970 *Positively Black.* Englewood Cliffs, N.J.: Prentice-Hall.

APTHEKER, HERBERT
1974 "Heavenly Days in Dixie or, The Time of Their Lives." *Political Affairs* (June/July).

BARATZ, JOAN, and ROGER SHUY, eds.
1969 *Teaching Black Children to Read.* Washington, D.C.: Center for Applied Linguistics.

BARATZ, STEPHEN
1970 "Social Science's Conceptualization of the Afro-American." In *Black America*, edited by John F. Szwed. New York: Basic Books.

BARATZ, STEPHEN, and JOAN BARATZ
1970 "Early Childhood Intervention: The Social Science Base of Institutional Racism." *Harvard Educational Review* 40: 29–50.

BERGER, BENNETT M.
1967 "Soul Searching." Review of *Urban Blues*, by Charles Keil. *Trans-action* 4 (7): 54–57.

BERNARD, SYDNEY B.
1964 *Fatherless Families: Their Economic and Social Adjustment.* Brandeis University Papers in Social Welfare, No. 7. Waltham, Mass.

BERREMAN, GERALD D.
1968 "Is Anthropology Alive? Social Responsibility in Social Anthropology." *Current Anthropology* 9: 391–96.

BOTT, ELIZABETH
1971 *Family and Social Network: Roles, Norms, and External Relationships in Ordinary Urban Families.* New York: Free Press.

CAPLOVITZ, DAVID
1963 *The Poor Pay More: Consumer Practices of Low-Income Families.* New York: Macmillan.

CLAIRMONT, DONALD H., and DENNIS W. MAGILL
    1974 *Africville: The Life and Death of a Canadian Black Community.* Toronto: McClelland & Stewart.

CROWLEY, DANIEL J.
    1971 "African Folktales in Afro-America." In *Black America*, edited by John F. Szwed. New York: Basic Books.

DOLLARD, JOHN
    1937 *Caste and Class in a Southern Town.* New Haven: Yale University Press.

DRAKE, ST. CLAIR
    1966 "The Social and Economic Status of the Negro in the United States." In *The Negro American*, edited by Talcott Parsons and Kenneth B. Clark. Boston: Houghton Mifflin.

DU BOIS, W. E. B.
    1899 *The Philadelphia Negro: A Social Study.* Philadelphia: University of Pennsylvania.
    1903 *The Souls of Black Folk.* Chicago: McClurg.
    1909 *The Negro American Family.* Atlanta: Atlanta University Press.

ELDER, LONNE
    1975 Interview, *New York Times*, Arts and Leisure, January 5.

FOGEL, ROBERT W., and STANLEY L. ENGERMAN
    1974 *Time on the Cross: The Economics of American Negro Slavery.* Boston: Little, Brown.

FRAZIER, E. FRANKLIN
    1957a *The Negro in the United States.* New York: Macmillan.
    1957b *Black Bourgeoisie.* New York: Free Press.

GLAZER, NATHAN, and DANIEL P. MOYNIHAN
    1963 *Beyond the Melting Pot: The Negroes, Puerto Ricans, Jews, Italians and Irish of New York City.* Cambridge: M.I.T. Press.

GOFFMAN, ERVING
    1959 *The Presentation of Self in Everyday Life.* Garden City, N.Y.: Doubleday.
    1961 *Asylums.* Garden City, N.Y.: Doubleday.
    1963 *Behavior in Public Places: Notes on the Social Organization of Gatherings.* New York: Free Press.

GOUGH, KATHLEEN
    1968 "New Proposals for Anthropologists." *Current Anthropology* 9: 403–407.

GOULDNER, ALVIN W.
    1970 *The Coming Crisis of Western Sociology.* New York: Basic Books.

HANNERZ, ULF
  1969   *Soulside: Inquiries into Ghetto Culture and Community.* New York: Columbia University Press.

HARRINGTON, MICHAEL
  1962   *The Other America: Poverty in the United States.* New York: Macmillan.

HASKELL, THOMAS L.
  1975   "The True and Tragical History of *Time on the Cross.*" Review of *Slavery and the Numbers Game: A Critique of "Time on the Cross."* by H. G. Gutman; "A Symposium on *Time on the Cross,*" by G. M. Walton, in *Explorations in Economic History,* vol. 12; and *Reckoning with Slavery: Critical Essays in the Quantitative History of American Negro Slavery,* by P. A. David et al. *New York Review of Books* 22 (15): 33–39.

HEER, DAVID M., ed.
  1968   *Social Statistics and the City: Report of a Conference.* Cambridge: Harvard University Press.

HERSKOVITS, MELVILLE J.
  1941   *The Myth of the Negro Past.* New York: Harper.

HIPPLER, ARTHUR E.
  1974   *Hunter's Point: A Black Ghetto.* New York: Basic Books.

HOWELL, JOSEPH T.
  1973   *Hard Living on Clay Street: Portraits of Blue Collar Families.* New York: Anchor Books.

HURSTON, ZORA N.
  1935   *Mules and Men.* Philadelphia: Lippincott.

HYMES, DELL, ed.
  1972   *Reinvesting Anthropology.* New York: Random House.

IANNI, FRANCIS A. J.
  1974   *Black Mafia: Ethnic Succession in Organized Crime.* New York: Simon & Schuster.

JACKSON, JUANITA, SABRA SLAUGHTER, and J. HERMAN BLAKE
  1974   "The Sea Islands as a Cultural Resource." *Black Scholar* (March): 32–39.

KEIL, CHARLES
  1966   *Urban Blues.* Chicago: University of Chicago Press.

KEMPTON, MURRAY
  1969   "The Cost of Being Black." *New York Times*, March 5.

LEACOCK, ELEANOR, ed.
  1971   *The Culture of Poverty: A Critique.* New York: Simon & Schuster.

LEE, EVERETT S.

1968 "Needed Improvements in Census Collection Procedures with Special Reference to the Disadvantaged." In *Social Statistics and the City*, edited by David M. Heer. Cambridge: Harvard University Press.

LEWIS, OSCAR

1966a "The Culture of Poverty." *Scientific American* 215 (4): 19–25.

1966b *La Vida: A Puerto Rican Family in the Culture of Poverty.* New York: Random House.

1967 *"The Children of Sanchez, Pedro Martinez* and *La Vida:* A CA Book Review." *Current Anthropology* 8: 480–500.

LIEBOW, ELLIOT

1967 *Tally's Corner: A Study of Negro Streetcorner Men.* Boston: Little, Brown.

MATZA, DAVID

1966 "The Disreputable Poor." In *Social Structure and Mobility in Economic Development*, edited by Neil J. Smelser and Seymour M. Lipset. Chicago: Aldine.

MCWORTER, GERALD

1969 "Deck the Ivey Racist Halls: The Case of Black Studies." In *Black Studies in the University*, edited by Armstead L. Robinson et al. New Haven: Yale University Press.

MILLER, S. M., and PAMELA ROBY

1970 *The Future of Inequality.* New York: Basic Books.

MILLER, WALTER B.

1958 "Lower Class Culture as a Generating Milieu of Gang Delinquency." *Journal of Social Issues* 14: 5–19.

1964 Foreword to *Fatherless Families*, by Sydney B. Bernard. Brandeis University Papers in Social Welfare, No. 7. Waltham, Mass.

MILNER, CHRISTINA and RICHARD

1972 *Black Players: The Secret World of Black Pimps.* Boston: Little, Brown.

MOYNIHAN, DANIEL P.

1965 *The Negro Family: The Case for National Action.* Washington, D.C.: U.S. Department of Labor.

1966 "Employment, Income, and the Ordeal of the Negro Family." In *The Negro American*, edited by Talcott Parsons and Kenneth B. Clark. Boston: Houghton Mifflin.

1967 "The President and the Negro: The Moment Lost." *Commentary* 43: 31–45.

MYRDAL, GUNNAR
   1962   *An American Dilemma.* Twentieth anniversary ed. New York:
          Harper & Row.

NATIONAL ADVISORY COMMISSION ON CIVIL DISORDERS
   1968   *Report of the National Advisory Commission on Civil Disorders*
          (Kerner Commission Report). New York: Dutton.

PARSONS, TALCOTT, and KENNETH B. CLARK, eds.
   1966   *The Negro American.* The Daedalus Library, vol. 7. Boston:
          Houghton Mifflin.

PERLEZ, JANE
   1973   "Alcohol and Meth: A New Peril." *New York Post,* December 6.

PORTER, SYLVIA
   1969   "Negro Women and Jobs." *New York Post,* August 5.

POWDERMAKER, HORTENSE
   1939   *After Freedom: A Cultural Study in the Deep South.* New York:
          Viking.
   1966   *Stranger and Friend: The Way of an Anthropologist.* New York:
          Norton.

PRITZKER, LEON, and N. D. ROTHWELL
   1968   "Procedural Difficulties in Taking Past Censuses in Predomi-
          nantly Negro, Puerto Rican, and Mexican Areas." In *Social
          Statistics and the City,* edited by David M. Heer. Cambridge:
          Harvard University Press.

ROBINSON, ARMSTEAD L., ET AL., eds.
   1969   *Black Studies in the University: A Symposium.* New Haven:
          Yale University Press.

RYAN, WILLIAM
   1965   "Savage Discovery: The Moynihan Report." *The Nation,*
          November 22.

SIEGEL, JACOB S.
   1968   "Completeness of Coverage of the Non-White Population in the
          1960 Census and Current Estimates, and Some Implications,"
          In *Social Statistics and the City,* edited by David M. Heer.
          Cambridge: Harvard University Press.

SMELSER, NEIL J., and SEYMOUR M. LIPSET, eds.
   1966   *Social Structure and Mobility in Economic Development.*
          Chicago: Aldine.

STACK, CAROL B.
   1974   *All Our Kin: Strategies for Survival in a Black Community.*
          New York: Harper & Row.

STEWART, WILLIAM
   1965 "Urban Negro Speech: Sociolinguistic Factors Affecting English
         Teaching." In *Social Dialects and Language Learning*, edited
         by R. W. Shuy. Champaign, Ill.: National Council of Teachers
         of English.
SZWED, JOHN F., ed.
   1970 *Black America*. New York: Basic Books.
SZWED, JOHN F.
   1974 "An American Anthropological Dilemma: The Politics of Afro-
         American Culture." In *Reinventing Anthropology*, edited by
         Dell Hymes. New York: Random House.
TAEUBER, KARL, and ALMA TAEUBER
   1965 *Negroes in Cities: Residential Segregation and Neighborhood
         Change*. Chicago: University of Chicago Press.
THOMPSON, EDGAR, ed.
   1939 *Race Relations and the Race Problem*. Durham, N.C.: Duke
         University Press.
Trans-action, eds.
   1968 "The Census: What's Wrong With It, and What Can Be Done
         About It." *Trans-action* 5 (6): 49–56.
U.S. BUREAU OF THE CENSUS
   n.d. *Confidential . . . Census Confidentiality . . . How It Grew*.
         Washington, D.C.: Government Printing Office.
   n.d. *All the Census People Can Do Is Count, Not Talk*. Washing-
         ton, D.C.: Government Printing Office.
   n.d. *Make Black Count*. Washington, D.C.: Government Printing
         Office.
VALENTINE, CHARLES A.
   1968 *Culture and Poverty: Critique and Counter-proposals*. Chicago:
         University of Chicago Press.
   1971 "Deficit, Difference, and Bicultural Models of Afro-American
         Behavior." *Harvard Educational Review* 41 (2): 137–57.
   1972 *Black Studies and Anthropology: Scholarly and Political Inter-
         ests in Afro-American Culture*. Reading, Mass.: Addison-
         Wesley.
VALENTINE, CHARLES A., and BETTYLOU VALENTINE
   1970 "Blackston: Progress Report on a Community Study in Urban
         Afro-America." Unpublished manuscript.
   1971 "Missing Men: A Comparative Methodological Study of Under-
         enumeration and Related Problems." Unpublished manuscript.

1972   "The Man and the Panthers: Explaining Away Revolutionaries
        with Suicide Theories." *Politics and Society* (Spring): 273; 286.

WARNER, W. LLOYD, and ALLISON DAVIS
  1939   "A Comparative Study of American Caste." In *Race Relations
          and the Race Problem*, edited by Edgar Thompson. Durham,
          N.C.: Duke University Press.

WARNER, W. LLOYD, and LEO SROLE
  1946   *The Social Systems of American Ethnic Groups*. New Haven:
          Yale University Press.

WHITTEN, NORMAN E., JR., and JOHN F. SZWED, eds.
  1970   *Afro-American Anthropology: Contemporary Perspectives on
          Theory and Research*. New York: Free Press.

WILLIS, WILLIAM S., JR.
  1974   "Skeletons in the Anthropological Closet." In *Reinvesting
          Anthropology*, edited by Dell Hymes. New York: Random
          House.

YOUNG, VIRGINIA H.
  1970   "Family and Childhood in a Southern Negro Community."
          American Anthropologist 72: 269–88.

INDEX